英単語ピーナツ
JUNIOR

大岩秀樹／佐藤誠司 ◆共著

PEANUT

南雲堂

協力者を紹介させていただきます。

安河内　哲也先生 ・ 清水　かつぞー先生

英文校閲
Jim Knudsen
Richard Best

校正協力
田平　稔

作詞
川村　徹

イラスト
はまの　ふみこ

カバー・本文デザイン
銀月堂

ナレーター
Josh Keller (米)
彼方　悠璃

制作
柴崎　利恵
日本ハイコム (株)
(有) 松村製本所

編集
加藤　敦

ありがとうございました。

まえがき

　英語を学ぶのはなぜなのでしょうか？

　学校の成績のため，進学のため，資格試験をとるため，就職のため，海外を視野に入れた活動をするため。中には，楽しいから趣味として，海外に友人を作りたいから，海外旅行をしたいからという人もいるでしょう。では，その中で英語を学ぶ理由として本当の正解はどれなのでしょうか？

　正解は，「全部」と言えるでしょう。現実的には成績や受験などに必要なものですし，仕事でも旅行でもボランティアでも，海外での活動を視野に入れれば，英語を扱う力は必要不可欠であることはもはや言う必要もないほど浸透した事実ですよね。

　それが事実であるならば，もしあなたが「○○のため」という何か1つの目的を意識した英語の学習をしていたとしたならば，そのような学習は昨日までにしませんか。

　英語を学ぶということは，単語を1つ覚えるたびに，世界中とつながっていくということなのです。英語を学ぶということは，表現1つが使えるようになるたびに，世界中とつながっていくということなのです。こんなすごいもの，英語以外にありますか!?　少なくとも，私は英語以外にはこんなにもすごいものを知りません。

　ピー単は「使える表現」として単語を身に付ける画期的な単語帳です。表現1つを覚えるごとに，世界とつながっていくイメージを強く持ちましょう。そうすれば近い将来，世界中と強くつながって

いる自分がいることに気づくことでしょう。さあ，そろそろ出発の時間のようです。

　　旅立ちましょう，世界へ！　あなたの本当の舞台へ！

大岩　秀樹

この本の使い方 by 安河内哲也

★ピーナツ方式で，一気に1441語を食べてしまおう！

　ピーナツには豆が2つ入っていますね。『英単語ピーナツ』も「形容詞＋名詞」や「動詞＋名詞」などの2語の連語からできています。

　たとえば「今度の月曜日」という意味の next Monday というフレーズには，next（次の）という形容詞と Monday（月曜日）という名詞の2つの単語が含まれています。このようなカタマリのことをコロケーションと呼びますが，ひとつのコロケーションを学習すると，2つの単語をいっぺんにおぼえることができるわけです。

　また，英文を素早く話したり書いたりするには，単語と単語をまとめてスピーディーに運用することが重要です。

　本書では，このような，英単語のピーナツ，つまり連語が，1ページに10個，全部で777個入っています。

　777個といっても，一つ一つの連語には複数の単語が含まれているわけですから，この1冊（JUNIORコース）で，合計1441個（INDEX収録語数）の英単語をマスターすることができるわけです。

★様々な学習法を組み合わせれば効果は倍増だ！

　本書と音声CDを使えば，様々な形式の学習が可能になります。英単語を暗記するには，あまり形式を固定せずに，マンネリ化を避けることも重要です。ここでは，ピーナツを使った様々な勉強方法を紹介したいと思います。（CDは10個ごとに録音されています）

1．日本語 → 英語【英作文方式】（もっとも標準的な学習法）

　日本語→英語の流れで食べていきます。単語のスペリングを2字か3字ヒントとして与えてありますから，これを頼りに全体のスペリングを思い出してください。頭の中でやってもかまいませんが，最初のうちは紙に書いていくことを勧めます。わからない単語は，左側のABC順に並んだお助けリストから選んで，素直に書き写しましょう。書き写す際に英単語を音読するとさらに頭に残ります。答えは裏のページにあります。ヒントだけで食べられたピーナツには，印をつけておきましょう。8ページの見本にあるように，正の字を書いてもいいし，日本語の周囲を線で囲んでもいいでしょう。

　この学習法にピッタリの日本語→英語の流れの音声データを別途ダウンロード販売(本体価格400円)しています。デジタルオーディオプレーヤーなどに入れて持ち歩き，777個のピーナツを完全に消化してしまいましょう。

Nan'Un-Do's STORE　https://nanundo.stores.jp/　『英単語ピーナツ』で検索！

🛒 STORES.jp

2．英語 → 日本語【即答通訳方式】

　英語に強くなるには，スピードを磨くことが大切です。連語を先に英語で見て，日本語に変換する練習をしてみましょう。この練習をするときには,「ピー単」を反対側からめくっていくとよいでしょう。日本語はわざわざ紙に書く必要はないでしょう。口頭で言ってみたり，頭の中でやってみて，できなかったものにチェックを入れていき，次の回はその連語を集中的に復習しましょう。

3．音声 → 日本語【口頭通訳方式】

　本書に付属の CD を用いて通訳訓練をやってみましょう。耳で聞いた英語をすぐに日本語にする訓練をします。最初は本の英語を見ながらでも大丈夫ですが，最終的には，耳だけで英語を聞きながら，日本語の意味がすべて出てくるようになるまで練習しましょう。

4．音声 → リピート【英英直解方式】

　発音の練習と英語のまま意味を理解する訓練をかねて，英語の音声をリピートしましょう。英語のまま概念が頭の中に描けるようになることが，最終的な目標となります。日常的にこの訓練を繰り返すことにより，英語の感覚が頭の中に定着していきます。また，英語を反射的に発話する訓練にも最適です。

★さあ，それでは早速ピーナツを食べ始めましょう！

◀アク →アクセント注意　　◀発音 →発音注意を示す

※発音は原則として米語音を採用。
※イタリック［斜体字］部分は省略可能。なおイタリックは次の場合も含む。

脱落
綴り字にはあっても，自然に発音すると過半数の英米人が脱落させる子音。
例：empty［ém*p*ti］

挿入
suggest, often 等の綴り字にあっても以前は発音されなかったが，最近（英または米で）半数を超えて発音されるようになった［g］および［t］等の挿入子音。

時

やあ、いらっしゃい

1	今度の月曜日
	n..t M..day

2	今週の火曜日
	t..s T...day

3	水曜日の晩に
	on W.....day e...ing

4	木曜日の夜に
	on T....day ni..t

5	金曜日を除いて
	ex...t F..day

6	土曜日は休みだ
	have S....day o.f

7	毎週日曜日に
	e...y S..day

8	おととい
	the day be...e ye....day

9	あさって
	the day a..er to....ow

10	今日の正午に
	at n..n t...y

after
before
evening
every
except
Friday
Monday
next
night
noon
off
Saturday
Sunday
this
Thursday
today
tomorrow
Tuesday
Wednesday
yesterday

 CD 2

1. **next Monday**
   |nékst| |mʌ́ndeɪ|

2. **this Tuesday**
   |tjúːzdeɪ|

3. **on Wednesday evening**
   |wénzdeɪ| ◀発音 |íːvnɪŋ|

4. **on Thursday night**
   |θə́ːrzdeɪ| |náɪt|

5. **except Friday**
   |ɪksépt| ◀アク |fráɪdeɪ|

6. **have Saturday off**
   |sǽtərdeɪ|

7. **every Sunday**
   |évri| |sʌ́ndeɪ|

8. **the day before yesterday**
   |bɪfɔ́ːr| |jéstərdeɪ|

9. **the day after tomorrow**
   |ǽftər| |təmɑ́ːroʊ|

10. **at noon today**
    |núːn| |tədéɪ|

10

| 初めましてピー君です |

ago
few
following
half
hour
just
little
minute
moment
month
now
per
second
since
then
thirty
wait
week
while
within

11	２，３日前 a f.w days a.o
12	たった今 j..t n.w
13	少しの間 for a li...e wh..e
14	少しの間待つ w..t for a m...nt
15	そのときからずっと si..e t..n
16	30分間 for h..f an h..r
17	30分間 for th..ty mi...es
18	１秒につき p.r se...d
19	１週間以内に wi..in a w..k
20	翌月 the fo....ing m..th

CD 3

| 11 | **a few days ago** |
| | [fjúː] [əɡóʊ] |

| 12 | **just now** |
| | [dʒʌ́st] [náʊ] |

| 13 | **for a little while** |
| | [lítl] [wáɪl] |

| 14 | **wait for a moment** |
| | [wéɪt] [móʊmənt] ◀発音 |

| 15 | **since then** |
| | [síns] [ðén] |

| 16 | **for half an hour** |
| | [hǽf] [áʊər] ◀発音 |

| 17 | **for thirty minutes** |
| | [θɔ́ːrti] [mínəts] ◀発音 |

| 18 | **per second** |
| | [pər] [sékənd] |

| 19 | **within a week** |
| | [wɪðín] ◀アク [wíːk] |

| 20 | **the following month** |
| | [fάːloʊɪŋ] [mʌ́nθ] |

21	長期間	a l..g pe..od
22	去年の春	l..t s..ing
23	１年中	a.l the y..r ar...d
24	もう一度	o..e ag..n
25	ふだんより遅く	la..r t..n us..l
26	今夜９時に	at nine o'c...k t...ght
27	深夜まで	u..il m..night
28	既に終わっている	have al...dy e.ded
29	時計塔[台]	a cl..k t..er
30	遅かれ早かれ	so..er or l..er

ピー単の案内役です

again
all
already
around
clock
end
last
later
later
long
midnight
once
o'clock
period
sooner
spring
than
tonight
tower
until
usual
year

CD 4

21 **a long period**
[lɔ́:ŋ]　[píəriəd] ◀発音

22 **last spring**
[lǽst]　[spríŋ]

23 **all the year around**
　　　　[jíər]　[əráund]

24 **once again**
[wʌ́ns]　[əgén]

25 **later than usual**
[léɪtər]　　　[júːʒuəl]

26 **at nine o'clock tonight**
　　　　　[əklɑ́:k]　[tənáɪt] ◀アク

27 **until midnight**
[əntíl]　[mídnàɪt] ◀アク

28 **have already ended**
　　　　[ɔːlrédi] ◀アク [éndɪd]

29 **a clock tower**
　　　　　[táʊər] ◀発音

30 **sooner or later**
[súːnər]

英語 English

準備運動忘れずに！

autumn
beginning
celebrate
century
Christmas
date
daytime
during
end
February
festival
fix
forever
January
last
late
spend
teen
twentieth
weekend

31	週末を過ごす
	sp..d a we...nd

32	昼間に
	d..ing the d..time

33	日付を確定する
	f.x the d..e

34	十代後半
	the l..e te..s

35	永遠に続く
	l..t fo...er

36	秋祭り
	an au..mn fe....al

37	クリスマスを祝う
	cel...ate Chri..mas

38	20世紀
	the twen...th ce...ry

39	1月末
	the e.d of Ja...ry

40	2月の初め
	the be....ing of Fe...ary

CD 5

31 **spend a weekend**
[spénd]　　[wíːkènd]

32 **during the daytime**
[dɔ́ːrɪŋ]　　[déɪtàɪm]

33 **fix the date**
[fíks]　　[déɪt]

34 **the late teens**
[tíːnz]

35 **last forever**
[lǽst]　[fərévər] ◀アク

36 **an autumn festival**
[ɔ́ːtəm] ◀発音　[féstəvl] ◀発音

37 **celebrate Christmas**
[séləbrèɪt] ◀アク　[krísməs] ◀発音

38 **the twentieth century**
[twéntiəθ] ◀発音　[séntʃəri]

39 **the end of January**
[dʒǽnjuèri]

40 **the beginning of February**
[bɪɡínɪŋ] ◀アク　[fébruəri]

英語
English

まずはあせらず
ゆっくりと

41	3月5日
□□□	Ma..h fi..h

42	エイプリルフール（4月1日）
□□□	A..il F..l's day

43	5月4日
□□□	M.y fo..th

44	6月の花嫁（はなよめ）
□□□	a J..e b..de

April
August
bride
dancer
December
eighth
fifth
fool
fourth
height
July
June
March
May
ninth
November
October
September
seventh
sixth

45	7月から8月まで
□□□	from J..y to Au...t

46	9月6日
□□□	Sep...ber si..h

47	10月7日
□□□	Oc...er sev...h

48	11月8日
□□□	No...ber ei...h

49	12月9日
□□□	De...ber ni..h

50	そのダンサーの身長　数量
□□□	the da..er's h..ght

CD 6

41 **March fifth**
[máːrtʃ] [fífθ]

42 **April Fool's day**
[éɪprəl] [fúːlz]

43 **May fourth**
[méɪ] [fɔ́ːrθ]

44 **a June bride**
[dʒúːn] [bráɪd]

45 **from July to August**
[dʒuláɪ] [ɔ́ːgəst] ◀発音

46 **September sixth**
[septémbər] [síksθ]

47 **October seventh**
[ɑːktóubər] ◀発音 [sévnθ]

48 **November eighth**
[nouvémbər] [éɪtθ] ◀発音

49 **December ninth**
[dɪsémbər] [náɪnθ]

50 **the dancer's height**
[dǽnsərz] [háɪt] ◀発音

age
banana
bridge
double
dozen
egg
Germany
length
lot
low
many
package
population
price
size
thing
thousand
twice
weight
year

51	橋の長さ
	the le...h of a br..ge

52	荷物の重さ
	the we..ht of a pa...ge

53	ドイツの人口
	the po...ation of Ge..any

54	千年
	a th...and y..rs

55	多くのもの
	m..y t..ngs

56	たくさんのバナナ
	a l.t of ba...as

57	２ダースの卵
	two do..n e..s

58	２倍の大きさ
	do..le the s..e

59	私の年齢の２倍
	t..ce my a.e

60	安値で
	at a l.w p..ce

 CD 7

51 **the length of a bridge**
[léŋkθ]　　　　　[brídʒ]

52 **the weight of a package**
[wéɪt] ◀発音　　　[pǽkɪdʒ]

53 **the population of Germany**
[pὰ:pjəléɪʃən]　　　[dʒɔ́ːrməni]

54 **a thousand years**
[θáuzn*d*]

55 **many things**
[méni]　　[θíŋz]

56 **a lot of bananas**
[bənǽnəz] ◀アク

57 **two dozen eggs**
[dʌ́zn] ◀発音

58 **double the size**
[dʌ́bl] ◀発音　　[sáɪz]

59 **twice my age**
[twáɪs]　　[éɪdʒ]

60 **at a low price**
[lóu]　　[práɪs]

英 語
English

billion
daughter
dollar
fifty
forty
happy
hundred
less
marriage
marry
member
meter
million
more
most
people
percent
point
than
yen
zero

61 100万ドル
a mi...on do...rs

62 50億円
five bi...on y.n

63 50パーセント
fi..y pe...nt

64 100より多く
m..e t..n a hu..red

65 40以下
fo..y or l..s

66 0.8メートル
z..o po..t eight me..rs

67 ほとんどの人々
m..t pe...e

68 会員の大部分
m..t of the me..ers

69 幸福な結婚
a ha..y ma...age

70 彼の娘と結婚する
m...y his da...ter

家族

CD 8

61 a million dollars
|míljən| |dá:lərz|

62 five billion yen
|bíljən| |jén|

63 fifty percent
|fífti| |pərsént|

64 more than a hundred
|hʌ́ndrəd|

65 forty or less
|fɔ́:rti|

66 zero point eight meters
|zíərou| |mí:tərz| ◀発音

67 most people
|móust| |pí:pl| ◀発音

68 most of the members
|mémbərz|

69 a happy marriage
|mǽrɪdʒ| ◀発音

70 marry his daughter
|mǽri| |dɔ́:tər| ◀発音

英語
English

毎日1分でも続けることが大切！

71	結婚している夫婦
□□□	a ma...ed co..le

72	彼女の前の夫
□□□	her fo..er hu..and

73	独身生活
□□□	a si..le l..e

74	前の男友だち
□□□	my pr...ous boyf...nd

75	女友だちを招待する
□□□	in..te a g..lfriend

76	大家族
□□□	a la..e fa...y

77	赤ちゃんの誕生
□□□	the b..th of a b..y

78	祖母を訪ねる
□□□	v..it my g...dmother

79	双子の姉妹
□□□	t..n si...rs

80	両親を尊敬する
□□□	re...ct my pa...ts

baby
birth
boyfriend
couple
family
former
girlfriend
grandmother
husband
invite
large
life
married
parent
previous
respect
single
sister
twin
visit

CD 9

71	**a married couple**
	[mǽrid]　　　[kʌ́pl] ◀発音

72	**her former husband**
	[fɔ́ːrmər]　　[hʌ́zbənd]

73	**a single life**
	[síŋgl]　　[láɪf]

74	**my previous boyfriend**
	[príːviəs] ◀発音　[bɔ́ɪfrènd] ◀アク

75	**invite a girlfriend**
	[ɪnváɪt] ◀アク　[gə́ːrlfrènd]

76	**a large family**
	[láːrdʒ]

77	**the birth of a baby**
	[bə́ːrθ]　　　[béɪbi]

78	**visit my grandmother**
	[vízət]　　　[grǽnmʌ̀ðər] ◀アク

79	**twin sisters**
	[twín]

80	**respect my parents**
	[rɪspékt] ◀アク　[péərənts] ◀発音

24

英語 English

あっ，英語で言えちゃった

81	私の兄
	my b.g br...er

82	いとこの名前
	my co..in's n..e

83	彼の高齢（こうれい）の祖父
	his a.ed g...dfather

84	父の時計
	my fa..er's w...h

85	母の代わりに
	in..ead of my mo..er

86	経営者の妻
	the ma..ger's w..e

87	成長して俳優（はいゆう）になる
	g..w up to be an ac..r

88	金持ちに生まれる
	be bo.n r..h

89	貧しい農民
	a p..r fa..er

90	裕福（ゆうふく）だ
	be w..l o.f

actor
aged
big
born
brother
cousin
farmer
father
grandfather
grow
instead
manager
mother
name
off
poor
rich
watch
well
wife

お金・買い物

 CD 10

81 **my big brother**

82 **my cousin's name**
[kʌ́znz] ◀発音

83 **his aged grandfather**
[éɪdʒɪd]　[grǽnfɑ̀:ðər]

84 **my father's watch**

85 **instead of my mother**
[ɪnstéd] ◀発音

86 **the manager's wife**
　　　[mǽnɪdʒərz] ◀アク [wáɪf]

87 **grow up to be an actor**
[gróʊ]　　　　　　　　[ǽktər]

88 **be born rich**
[bɔ́:rn]　[rítʃ]

89 **a poor farmer**
[púər]◀発音[fɑ́:rmər]

90 **be well off**

英語 English

ここから全てが始まるんだなあ

91	安い給料
	a l.w sa..ry

92	税金を支払う
	p.y a t.x

93	大金を稼ぐ
	ma.e m..h mo..y

94	財布を落とす
	d..p my wa..et

95	キャッシュカード
	a c..h c..d

96	買い物袋
	a sh...ing b.g

97	値下げ販売
	a dis...nt s..e

98	無料の飲み物
	a f..e d...k

99	必要経費
	nece...ry c..t

100	小銭
	s..ll ch...e

bag
card
cash
change
cost
discount
drink
drop
free
low
make
money
much
necessary
pay
salary
sale
shopping
small
tax
wallet

○ CD 11

91	**a low salary** [sǽləri]
92	**pay a tax** [péɪ]
93	**make much money** [mʌ́ni]
94	**drop my wallet** [drάːp]　　[wάːlət] ◀発音
95	**a cash card**
96	**a shopping bag**
97	**a discount sale** [dískaʊnt]　　[séɪl]
98	**a free drink**
99	**necessary cost** [nésəsèri] ◀アク　[kɔ́(ː)st] ◀発音
100	**small change** [tʃéɪndʒ] ◀発音

100個 一気食いへの挑戦！

	挑戦日	所要時間	正答数
1	年　月　日	分　　秒	/100
2	年　月　日	分　　秒	/100
3	年　月　日	分　　秒	/100
4	年　月　日	分　　秒	/100
5	年　月　日	分　　秒	/100
6	年　月　日	分　　秒	/100
7	年　月　日	分　　秒	/100
8	年　月　日	分　　秒	/100
9	年　月　日	分　　秒	/100
10	年　月　日	分　　秒	/100

繰り返しは無限の喜びである

英単語つれづれ草

何のために勉強をしているのですか？

　あなたは何のために勉強をしているのですか？　資格試験のため？　入試のため？　そこに勉強があるから？　......実は私たちが勉強をする理由は人それぞれで，「このために勉強は必要なのだ」という絶対的な理由などないのだと思います。どんな理由にしても，やらなければいけないものではある。ならば，やりましょう。理由など気にせずに。

　しかしながら，やり続けなければ見えてこないものもある。ずっと勉強を続けたら，おそらく30歳くらいで，たくさんある解答の1つにたどり着くはずなのです。何のために勉強をするのか？

　「前へ進んでいくため。」

　これは間違いなく解答の1つに入っていると私は思う。私たち人間は，知識や経験がなければ何も生み出すことなどできない生物と言えるでしょう。これから先，一生懸命生きていけば，特に意識をしなくても素晴らしい経験を積み重ねていくことは可能でしょう。しかし，知識だけは，自らが求め，積み重ねようと努力をしなければ決して自分のものにはならないものなのです。

　社会人の多くは忙しい中でも前へ進むために必死で時間を確保し，勉強をしている。もし，あなたがまだ社会人ではないならば，今が絶好のチャンスなのだ。この時期に，どれだけの知識が蓄えられるかが，大きく人生を左右すると言っても過言ではない。今こそ，ピー単で，前へ，前へ，一歩でも前へ進む力をつけていきましょう。

英語
English

101	10円玉
	a 10-y.n c..n

102	20セント
	tw...y c...s

103	コンビニ
	a con...ience st..e

104	商品を売る
	s..l g...s

105	このサングラスがほしい
	want th..e sun...sses

106	安いハンドバッグ
	a ch..p ha...ag

107	高価な指輪
	an ex...sive r..g

108	貴重な宝石
	a pr...ous je..l

109	本物のダイヤモンド
	a r..l di...nd

110	贈り物を包む
	w..p a g..t

いつでも
どこでも
誰とでも

cent
cheap
coin
convenience
diamond
expensive
gift
goods
handbag
jewel
precious
real
ring
sell
store
sunglasses
these
twenty
wrap
yen

🔘 CD 12

101 **a 10-yen coin**

102 **twenty cents**
|twénti|

103 **a convenience store**
|kənvíːnjəns| ◀ア ク　|stɔ́ːr|

104 **sell goods**
|gúdz|

105 **want these sunglasses**
|ðíːz|　|sʌ́ŋglæ̀sɪz| ◀ア ク

106 **a cheap handbag**
|tʃíːp|

107 **an expensive ring**
|ɪkspénsɪv|

108 **a precious jewel**
|préʃəs| ◀発音　|dʒúːəl| ◀発音

109 **a real diamond**
|ríːjəl|　|dáɪmənd| ◀発音

110 **wrap a gift**
|rǽp| ◀発音

自分を信じることから始めよう！

answer
call
camera
cell
computer
digital
e-mail
exchange
hold
later
line
message
personal
phone
present
record
send
silent
telephone

電話・パソコンなど

111 贈(おく)り物を交(こう)換(かん)する
ex...nge pr...nts

112 携(けい)帯(たい)電話
a c..l ph..e

113 無言（の）電話
a si...t c..l

114 電話に出る
a...er the tel...one

115 電話を切らずに待つ
h..d the l..e

116 あなたに後で電話する
c..l you la..r

117 伝言を録音する
re...d a me...ge

118 （電子）メールを送る
s..d an e-m..l

119 デジカメ
a di...al ca..ra

120 パソコン
a pe...nal co...ter

33

CD 13

[111] **exchange presents**
|ɪkstʃéɪndʒ| [préznts] ◀アク

[112] **a cell phone**

[113] **a silent call**
|sáɪlənt|

[114] **answer the telephone**
|ǽnsər|

[115] **hold the line**
|hóʊld| |láɪn|

[116] **call you later**

[117] **record a message**
|rɪkɔ́ːrd| ◀アク [mésɪdʒ] ◀アク

[118] **send an e-mail**

[119] **a digital camera**
[dídʒətl]

[120] **a personal computer**
|pə́ːrsənl|

そうだ、ピー単やろう

121	かっこいいウェブサイト
□□□	a c..l we...te

122	ネットオークション
□□□	an In...net au..ion

123	インターネットで入手できる
□□□	be av...able on..ne

124	パスワードを忘れる
□□□	fo..et my pa...ord

125	郵便を受け取る
□□□	re...ve the m..l

126	手紙をポストに入れる
□□□	p..t a l...er

127	使用済みの切手
□□□	a u..d st..p

128	郵便局
□□□	a p..t o...ce

129	便利な道具
□□□	a con...ient t..l

130	色鉛筆（えんぴつ）
□□□	a c...r pe...l

auction
available
color
convenient
cool
forget
Internet
letter
mail
office
online
password
pencil
post
receive
stamp
tool
used
website

道具など

🅒 CD 14

121 **a cool website**
[kú:l]

122 **an Internet auction**
[íntərnèt] ◀アク [ɔ́:kʃən]

123 **be available online**
[əvéɪləbl]

124 **forget my password**
[fərgét]   [pǽswə̀:rd] ◀アク

125 **receive the mail**
[rɪsí:v]

126 **post a letter**
[póʊst] ◀発音

127 **a used stamp**
[jú:zd] ◀発音

128 **a post office**

129 **a convenient tool**
[kənví:njənt] ◀アク [tú:l] ◀発音

130 **a color pencil**
[kʌ́lər] ◀発音

英語
English

CDをまねて声を出そう！

131	はさみ一丁(いっちょう)
□□□	a p..r of sci...rs

132	１枚の紙
□□□	a sh..t of p...r

133	壁(かべ)のポスター
□□□	a po..er on the w..l

134	果物(くだもの)かご
□□□	a f...t b..ket

135	日用品
□□□	an ev...day i..m

136	たばこ入れ
□□□	a ci...ette c..e

137	きれいな人形
□□□	a pr...y d..l

138	ハンドバッグをなくす
□□□	l..e a p..se

139	カギを探す
□□□	l..k for a k.y

140	なくしたスマホを見つける
□□□	f..d a l..t smart...ne

basket
case
cigarette
doll
everyday
find
fruit
item
key
look
lose
lost
pair
paper
poster
pretty
purse
scissors
sheet
smartphone
wall

CD 15

131 **a pair of scissors**
[péər] ◀発音 [sízərz] ◀発音

132 **a sheet of paper**
[ʃíːt]

133 **a poster on the wall**
[póustər] ◀発音　　[wɔ́ːl]

134 **a fruit basket**
[frúːt]

135 **an everyday item**
[áɪtəm] ◀発音

136 **a cigarette case**
[sígərèt]　　[kéɪs]

137 **a pretty doll**
[príti] ◀発音 [dáːl] ◀発音

138 **lose a purse**
[lúːz] ◀発音 [pɔ́ːrs]

139 **look for a key**
[lúk]

140 **find a lost smartphone**
[fáɪnd]　　[lɔ́(ː)st]

英語 English

衣類

誰かに話しているつもりで！

141	いい服 f..e cl...es
142	ふだん着 ca...l w..r
143	きついスーツ a ti..t s..t
144	だぶだぶの上着 a lo..e ja..et
145	絹(きぬ)のネクタイ a s..k t.e
146	コートを着る p.t on my c..t
147	めがねをかけている w..r g...ses
148	リボンを結(むす)ぶ t.e a ri...n
149	かわいらしいドレス a ch...ing d..ss
150	ファッションモデル a fa...on m...l

casual
charming
clothes
coat
dress
fashion
fine
glasses
jacket
loose
model
put
ribbon
silk
suit
tie
tight
wear

CD 16

141. **fine clothes** [klóuz] ◀発音

142. **casual wear** [kǽʒuəl] [wéər]

143. **a tight suit** [táɪt] [súːt]

144. **a loose jacket** [lúːs] ◀発音

145. **a silk tie** [táɪ]

146. **put on my coat** [kóut] ◀発音

147. **wear glasses**

148. **tie a ribbon**

149. **a charming dress** [tʃáːrmɪŋ]

150. **a fashion model**

英語 English

英語を母国語だと思って発音しよう！

breakfast
brown
cap
clean
cloth
cotton
dirty
glove
hat
head
inside
laundry
pants
pocket
put
shoe
skip
skirt
sport
straw
thin
wash

151 綿のスカート
a co..on s...t

152 薄い布
t..n c..th

153 内ポケット
an in...e po...t

154 茶色の手袋
b...n g...es

155 運動靴
s...ts sh..s

156 汚れたズボンを洗う
w..h d..ty pa..s

157 きれいな洗濯物
c...n la...ry

158 麦わら帽子
a st..w h.t

159 帽子を頭にかぶる
p.t a c.p on my h..d

160 朝食を抜く
s..p bre...ast

食事

41

CD 17

151. **a cotton skirt**
 [ká:tn]　[skə́rt]

152. **thin cloth**
 [θín]　[klɔ́(:)θ]

153. **an inside pocket**

154. **brown gloves**
 [bráun]　[glʌ́vz] ◀発音

155. **sports shoes**
 [ʃú:z] ◀発音

156. **wash dirty pants**
 [wá:ʃ]　[də́:rti]

157. **clean laundry**
 [lɔ́:ndri] ◀発音

158. **a straw hat**
 [strɔ́:] ◀発音

159. **put a cap on my head**

160. **skip breakfast**
 [brékfəst] ◀発音

お酒はハタチになってから

161	昼食をとる
	h..e l..ch

162	軽い夕食
	a l...t su..er

163	夕食のしたくをする
	get d...er r..dy

164	空腹に感じる
	f..l h...ry

165	少しのどが渇(かわ)いている
	a b.t th...ty

166	何でも食べる
	e.t an...ing

167	何か飲むもの
	som...ing to d...k

168	食間に
	be...en m..ls

169	新鮮(しんせん)な野菜
	f...h ve...ables

170	三ツ星レストラン
	a three-s..r res...rant

anything
between
bit
dinner
drink
eat
feel
fresh
have
hungry
light
lunch
meal
ready
restaurant
something
supper
thirsty
three-star
vegetable

日本語
Japanese

CD 18

161 have lunch

162 a light supper
     |sʌ́pər|

163 get dinner ready
     |rédi|

164 feel hungry
     |fíːl| |hʌ́ŋgri| ◀発音

165 a bit thirsty
     |θə́ːrsti|

166 eat anything

167 something to drink

168 between meals
     |míːlz|

169 fresh vegetables
     |védʒtəblz|

170 a three-star restaurant
     |réstərənt| ◀発音

44

英語
English

3時のおやつに
ピー単10個！

171	メニューから選ぶ
	ch...e from a m..u

172	フランス料理を出す
	se..e F...ch d...es

173	特別なデザート
	a sp...al de...rt

174	豚肉より鶏肉を好む
	p...er ch...en to p..k

175	１杯のビール
	a g...s of b..r

176	１本のワイン
	a bo..le of w..e

177	もう１杯のお茶
	an...er c.p of t.a

178	誕生祝いのケーキ
	a bi...day c..e

179	１切れのステーキ
	a p...e of st..k

180	私にソースを手渡す
	p..s me the sa..e

another
beer
birthday
bottle
cake
chicken
choose
cup
dessert
dish
French
glass
menu
pass
piece
pork
prefer
sauce
serve
special
steak
tea
wine

CD 19

171 choose from a menu
|tʃúːz| ◀発音　　　　　|ménjuː|

172 serve French dishes
|sə́ːrv|

173 a special dessert
|dizə́ːrt| ◀発音◀アク

174 prefer chicken to pork
|prifə́ːr|　　　　　|pɔ́ːrk|

175 a glass of beer
|bíər| ◀発音

176 a bottle of wine

177 another cup of tea
|ənʌ́ðər|

178 a birthday cake
|bə́ːrθdèi|　　|kéik|

179 a piece of steak
|píːs|　　|stéik| ◀発音

180 pass me the sauce
|sɔ́ːs| ◀発音

英語 English

旅のおともに
ピー単1冊

181	すっぱいブドウ [負け惜しみ]
	s..r g...es

182	甘い香りがする
	s...l sw..t

183	おいしい味がする
	ta..e g..d

184	おいしいスープ
	a de...ious s..p

185	辛いカレー
	h.t c...y

186	苦いチョコレート
	b...er c...olate

187	パンを焼く
	b..e b...d

188	生のニンジン
	a r.w ca..ot

189	じゃがいもをゆでる
	b..l po...oes

190	チーズを切る
	c.t c...se

bake
bitter
boil
bread
carrot
cheese
chocolate
curry
cut
delicious
good
grape
hot
potato
raw
smell
soup
sour
sweet
taste

日本語
Japanese

CD 20

181 sour grapes
[sáuər] ◀発音 [gréɪps]

182 smell sweet
[smél]   [swíːt]

183 taste good
[téɪst]

184 a delicious soup
[dɪlíʃəs] ◀アク   [súːp] ◀発音

185 hot curry
[kə́ːri]

186 bitter chocolate
[bítər]   [tʃɑ́ːklət] ◀アク

187 bake bread
[béɪk]   [bréd]

188 a raw carrot
[rɔ́ː] ◀発音 [kǽrət]

189 boil potatoes
[bɔ́ɪl]   [pətéɪtouz] ◀発音

190 cut cheese
[kʌ́t]   [tʃíːz]

音読は絶対！

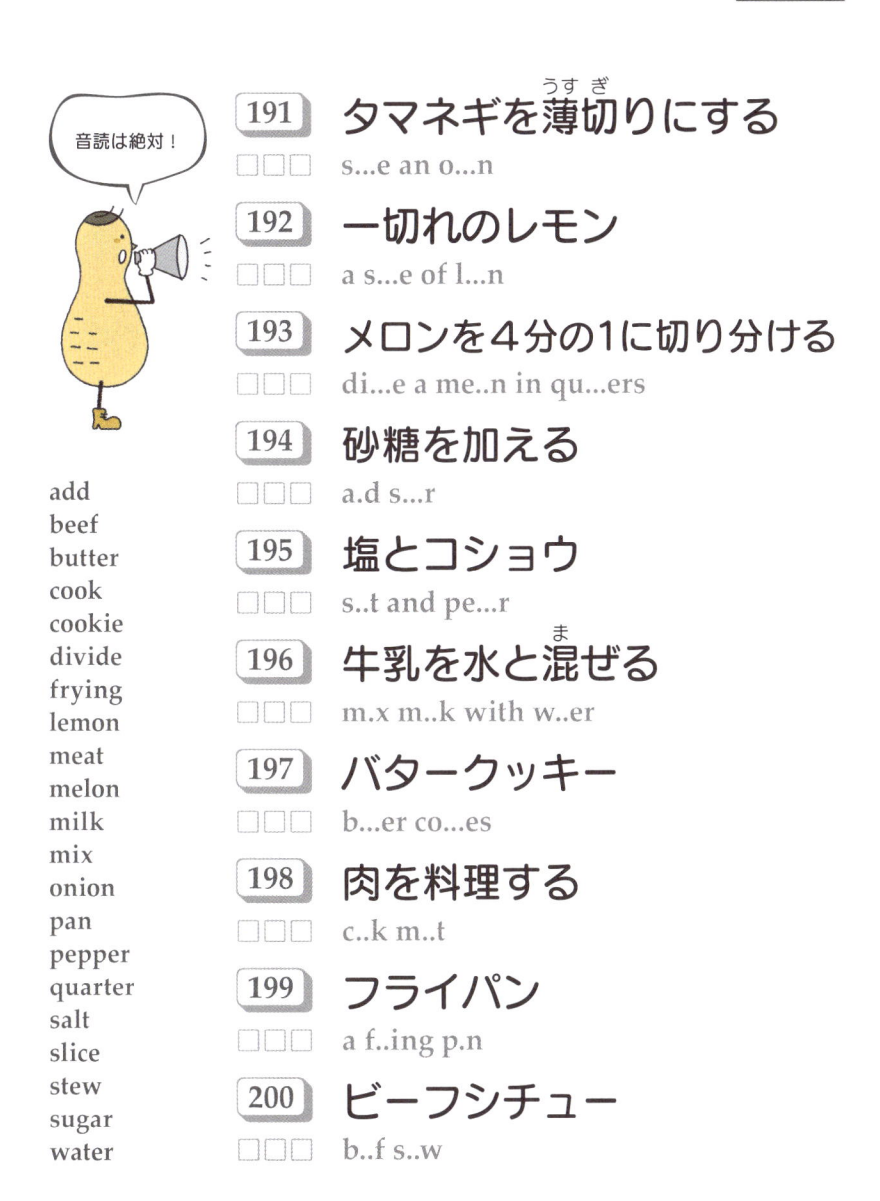

191	タマネギを薄切りにする
	s...e an o...n

192	一切れのレモン
	a s...e of l...n

193	メロンを4分の1に切り分ける
	di...e a me..n in qu...ers

194	砂糖を加える
	a.d s...r

195	塩とコショウ
	s..t and pe...r

196	牛乳を水と混ぜる
	m.x m..k with w..er

197	バタークッキー
	b...er co...es

198	肉を料理する
	c..k m..t

199	フライパン
	a f..ing p.n

200	ビーフシチュー
	b..f s..w

add
beef
butter
cook
cookie
divide
frying
lemon
meat
melon
milk
mix
onion
pan
pepper
quarter
salt
slice
stew
sugar
water

英語
English

CD 21

191 slice an onion
[sláɪs]　　[ʌ́njən] ◀発音

192 a slice of lemon
　　　　　　[lémən]

193 divide a melon in quarters
[dɪváɪd]　　　　　　[kwɔ́:rtərz]

194 add sugar
[ǽd]　[ʃúgər]

195 salt and pepper
[sɔ́:lt] ◀発音

196 mix milk with water

197 butter cookies
[bʌ́tər]　[kúkiz]

198 cook meat
　　　　[mí:t]

199 a frying pan

200 beef stew
[bí:f]　[stjú:] ◀発音

50

100個 一気食いへの挑戦！

挑戦日	所要時間	正答数
1 　年　月　日	分　　秒	/100
2 　年　月　日	分　　秒	/100
3 　年　月　日	分　　秒	/100
4 　年　月　日	分　　秒	/100
5 　年　月　日	分　　秒	/100
6 　年　月　日	分　　秒	/100
7 　年　月　日	分　　秒	/100
8 　年　月　日	分　　秒	/100
9 　年　月　日	分　　秒	/100
10 　年　月　日	分　　秒	/100

繰り返しは無限の喜びである

英単語つれづれ草

求められたより、さらに上をいけ！

　一生懸命頑張っているのに、なかなか周りの人に認めてもらえない。言われたとおりのことを、100％やっていても、それでも褒めてもらえない。そんな経験をしたことはありませんか？　まだ経験したことがないなら、それはきっと奇跡が起きているのかもしれません。私や私の友人はそんな経験ばかりでしたから。

　しかし、考えてみたら当たり前のことでした。自分も頑張っているけど、友人も頑張っている。よく見れば、みんなが頑張っている。自分だけが頑張っているわけじゃなかった。また、何かを言われて、100％で返せば「ありがとう」で終わるのは当たり前で、99％で返せば怒られることだってあった。考えれば考えるほど、当然だった。

　もし、あなたが人生の中で、だれかに認められたい、評価されたいと思う時があるなら、その思いを叶える方法は1つである。

　求められたことに対して120％の結果で応えること。

　それが相手を驚かせ、喜ばせ、感動させる。そして、認められ、評価される。もちろん、120％の結果を出すためには、短期的な努力ではなく、長期的に、いつ、何が起こっても大丈夫なように準備をしておく必要がある。

　英語に関して、今後の人生の中で、驚かせ、喜ばせ、感動してもらうために、ピー単で120％の結果が出せる準備をしておこう。

　求められたより、さらに上を行け。

英語 English

ていねいに何度でも！

201	アップルパイ an a...e p.e
202	トマトジュース to..to ju..e
203	手作りのパスタ home...e pa..a
204	柔(やわ)らかいキャンディー s..t ca..y
205	食卓(しょくたく)のしたくをする s.t the ta..e
206	とがったナイフ a sh..p k...e
207	サラダ用フォーク a sa..d f..k
208	皿を片付ける re..ve the p...es
209	台所の流し a ki...en s..k
210	閑静(かんせい)な地区 a c..m nei...orhood

apple
calm
candy
fork
homemade
juice
kitchen
knife
neighborhood
pasta
pie
plate
remove
salad
set
sharp
sink
soft
table
tomato

住居

CD 22

201 an apple pie
[ǽpl] [páɪ]

202 tomato juice
[təméɪtoʊ] ◀アク [dʒúːs]

203 homemade pasta
[hóʊmméɪd] [páːstə]

204 soft candy

205 set the table
[téɪbl]

206 a sharp knife
[ʃáːrp] [náɪf] ◀発音

207 a salad fork
[sǽləd] [fɔ́ːrk]

208 remove the plates
[rɪmúːv] [pléɪts]

209 a kitchen sink
[kítʃən]

210 a calm neighborhood
[káːm] ◀発音 [néɪbəhùd] ◀発音 ◀アク

声に出すと効果絶大！

211	間違った住所
	the w...g ad...ss

212	一人で暮らす
	l..e a...e

213	日当たりのいいアパート
	a su..y apart...t

214	おじの家に泊まる
	s..y with my u...e

215	家のない子ども
	a home...s k.d

216	家を建てる
	bu..d a h...e

217	屋根を修理する
	re...r a r..f

218	門の外側に
	out...e the g..e

219	表玄関
	the f...t p..ch

220	家にこもっている
	s..y at h..e

address
alone
apartment
build
front
gate
home
homeless
house
kid
live
outside
porch
repair
roof
stay
sunny
uncle
wrong

CD 23

211 **the wrong address**
|rɔ́(:)ŋ| |ədrés| ◀アク

212 **live alone**
|lív| |əlóun|

213 **a sunny apartment**
|sʌ́ni|

214 **stay with my uncle**
|ʌ́ŋkl|

215 **a homeless kid**

216 **build a house**
|bíld|

217 **repair a roof**
|rɪpéər| ◀発音 |rúːf|

218 **outside the gate**
|géɪt|

219 **the front porch**
|fránt|◀発音|pɔ́ːrtʃ|

220 **stay at home**

英語
English

ジェスチャーを付けて言ってみよう！

221	庭の世話をする
	t..e c..e of a ga..en

222	背の高い木
	a t..l t..e

223	塀にペンキを塗る
	p..nt a fe..e

224	暗い広間
	a d..k h..l

225	３階に
	on the th..d f...r

226	上の階の寝室
	a b...oom ups...rs

227	彼女を下の階へ連れて行く
	t..e her downs...rs

228	ドアをノックする
	k..ck on the d..r

229	大きな音
	a l..d n..se

230	騒がしい隣人
	a n...y nei...or

bedroom
care
dark
door
downstairs
fence
floor
garden
hall
knock
loud
neighbor
noise
noisy
paint
take
tall
third
tree
upstairs

日本語 / Japanese

CD 24

221 take care of a garden
[kéər]

222 a tall tree
[tɔ́:l]

223 paint a fence
[péɪnt]

224 a dark hall
[dá:rk] [hɔ́:l] ◀発音

225 on the third floor
[θə́:rd]

226 a bedroom upstairs
[ʌ́pstéərz]

227 take her downstairs
[dáʊnstéərz]

228 knock on the door
[ná:k] ◀発音

229 a loud noise
[láʊd] [nɔ́ɪz]

230 a noisy neighbor
[nɔ́ɪzi] [néɪbər] ◀発音

231	電気スタンド	a d..k l..p
232	木製の家具	wo...n fur...ure
233	火災報知器	a f..e a...m
234	空き缶	an e..ty c.n
235	テーブルの上の花びん	a v..e on the t...e
236	ベッドのそばに	be...e the b.d
237	お風呂のしたくをする	pre..re a b..h
238	壊れたシャワー	a b...en sh..er
239	ぬれたタオル	a w.t to..l
240	水が一杯入っている	be f..led with w...r

言葉に魂をこめて！

alarm
bath
bed
beside
broken
can
desk
empty
fill
fire
furniture
lamp
prepare
shower
table
towel
vase
water
wet
wooden

CD 25

231 **a desk lamp**
[lǽmp]

232 **wooden furniture**
[wúdn] ◀発音 [fə́ːrnɪtʃər] ◀発音

233 **a fire alarm**
[fáɪər] ◀発音 [əláːrm]

234 **an empty can**
[émpti]

235 **a vase on the table**
[véɪs] ◀発音

236 **beside the bed**
[bɪsáɪd]

237 **prepare a bath**
[prɪpéər] ◀発音 ◀アク

238 **a broken shower**
[bróʊkən] [ʃáʊər]

239 **a wet towel**
[táʊəl] ◀発音

240 **be filled with water**
[fíld]

英語 English

単語ができれば英語は通じる！

241	トイレを使う
	u.e a ba..room

242	トイレ用ブラシ
	a to...t b..sh

243	閉まっている窓
	a c...ed wi..ow

244	下の方の棚(たな)
	the l..er sh..f

245	厚(あつ)い毛布
	a th..k b...ket

246	カーテンの陰(かげ)に
	be...d the cu...in

247	床屋(とこや)の椅子(いす)
	a ba..er's ch..r

248	いつもの習慣(しゅうかん)
	my u..al ha..t

249	パーティーを開く
	h..d a p..ty

250	会合(かいごう)に欠席する
	be a..ent from a m...ing

absent
barber
bathroom
behind
blanket
brush
chair
closed
curtain
habit
hold
lower
meeting
party
shelf
thick
toilet
use
usual
window

生活一般

CD 26

241 **use a bathroom**
[bǽθrùːm] ◀アク

242 **a toilet brush**
[bráʃ]

243 **a closed window**
[klóʊzd] ◀発音

244 **the lower shelf**
[ʃélf]

245 **a thick blanket**
[θík]　　[blǽŋkət]

246 **behind the curtain**
[bɪháɪnd]　　[kə́ːrtn]

247 **a barber's chair**
[báːrbərz]　　[tʃéər]

248 **my usual habit**
[júːʒuəl]　　[hǽbət]

249 **hold a party**

250 **be absent from a meeting**
[ǽbsənt]

調子がよいときゃ もう一押し

251	正式な招待
	a fo..al inv...tion

252	訪問客を歓迎する
	we...me a vi...or

253	しばしば彼女に会う
	m..t her of..n

254	いいやつ［男］
	a n..e g.y

255	私の友人の１人
	a fr...d of m..e

256	固い友情
	a f..m frie...hip

257	ほっそりした少女
	a s..m g..l

258	内気な少年
	a s.y b.y

259	上品な婦人
	an e...ant l..y

260	年配の紳士
	an el...ly gen...man

boy
elderly
elegant
firm
formal
friend
friendship
gentleman
girl
guy
invitation
lady
meet
mine
nice
often
shy
slim
visitor
welcome

CD 27

251 **a formal invitation**
[fɔ́ːrml]   [ìnvətéɪʃən]

252 **welcome a visitor**
[wélkəm]

253 **meet her often**
[míːt]   [ɔ́ːfn]

254 **a nice guy**
[gáɪ] ◀発音

255 **a friend of mine**
[máɪn] ◀発音

256 **a firm friendship**
[fɔ́ːrm]

257 **a slim girl**
[slím]

258 **a shy boy**
[ʃáɪ]

259 **an elegant lady**
[éləgənt]   [léɪdi]

260 **an elderly gentleman**

英語 English

眠いときは思い切って寝よう！

avenue
away
bicycle
close
cross
cut
draw
far
frozen
highway
map
narrow
railroad
ride
road
short
sort
straight
street
woman

交通

261 あらゆる種類の女性
all s..ts of wo..n

262 細い通り
a na..ow st...t

263 まっすぐな幹線道路
a st...ght hi...ay

264 近道
a sh..t c.t

265 凍結した道路
a fr..en r..d

266 大通りの近くに
c..se to the a...ue

267 地図を描く
d..w a m.p

268 遠く離れて
f.r a..y

269 自転車に乗る
r..e a bi..cle

270 線路を渡る
cr..s a ra...oad

日本語 / Japanese

CD 28

261 all sorts of women
[sɔ́ːrts] [wímin] ◀発音

262 a narrow street
[nǽrou]

263 a straight highway
[stréɪt] ◀発音 [háɪwèɪ]

264 a short cut

265 a frozen road
[fróʊzn] [róʊd]

266 close to the avenue
[klóʊs] ◀発音 [ǽvənjùː] ◀アク

267 draw a map
[drɔ́ː] ◀発音

268 far away
[fɑ́ːr]

269 ride a bicycle
[ráɪd] [báɪsəkl] ◀発音

270 cross a railroad
[réɪlròʊd]

気がつけば,夢が英語になっているかも!?

around
carefully
corner
direction
downtown
drive
drive
driving
gas
green
hit
left
light
right
safe
sign
station
traffic
truck
turn

271 車で繁華街(はんかがい)へ行く
dr..e dow...wn

272 トラックにはねられる
be h.t by a tr..k

273 ガソリンスタンド
a g.s st..ion

274 安全運転
s..e dr..ing

275 慎重(しんちょう)に運転する
dr..e ca...ully

276 左へ曲がる
t..n l..t

277 角を曲がったところに
a...nd the co..er

278 交通標識(ひょうしき)
a tr...ic s..n

279 青信号
a g..en li..t

280 正しい方向に
in the ri..t di...tion

CD 29

271 drive downtown
|dráɪv|

272 be hit by a truck
|trʌ́k|

273 a gas station
|stéɪʃən|

274 safe driving

275 drive carefully
|kéərfəli|

276 turn left
|tə́ːrn| ◀発音

277 around the corner

278 a traffic sign
|trǽfɪk|◀アク |sáɪn| ◀発音

279 a green light

280 in the right direction
|dərékʃən|

思わなければ、実現しない！

281	タクシーの運転手
	a t..i dr..er

282	バス停
	a b.s s..p

283	急行列車
	an ex...ss tr..n

284	トンネルを通り抜ける
	go th...gh a tu..el

285	地下鉄の駅
	a su...y s...ion

286	人ごみの中に
	a..ng the cr..d

287	まもなく到着する
	ar..ve s..n

288	彼女を見送る
	s.e her o.f

289	急ぐ方がいい
	had be..er hu..y

290	向こうに
	o..r th..e

among
arrive
better
bus
crowd
driver
express
hurry
off
over
see
soon
station
stop
subway
taxi
there
through
train
tunnel

場所・地理

日本語
Japanese

 CD 30

281 **a taxi driver**

282 **a bus stop**

283 **an express train**
[Iksprés] ◀アク

284 **go through a tunnel**
[θrúː] ◀発音   [tʌnl] ◀発音

285 **a subway station**
[sʌ́bwèɪ]

286 **among the crowd**
[əmʌ́ŋ]   [kráud] ◀発音

287 **arrive soon**
[əráɪv]   [súːn]

288 **see her off**

289 **had better hurry**
[hə́ːri]

290 **over there**

	291	この近くに ar..nd h..e
	292	丘のふもとに at the f..t of a h..l
	293	岸に沿って a..ng the sh..e
	294	雲の上に a..ve the cl..ds
	295	地平線の下に be..w the ho...on
	296	広大な砂漠 a v..t de...t
	297	山に登る c...b a mo...ain
	298	幅の広い川 a w..e ri..r
	299	海に面している f..e the s.a
	300	平地 f..t l..d

above
along
around
below
climb
cloud
desert
face
flat
foot
here
hill
horizon
land
mountain
river
sea
shore
vast
wide

さあ,今日もやるぞっ!

CD 31

291 around here

292 at the foot of a hill
|fút| ◀発音

293 along the shore
|ʃɔ́ːr|

294 above the clouds
|əbʌ́v| ◀発音　　|kláʊdz|

295 below the horizon
|bɪlóʊ| ◀アク　　|həráɪzn| ◀アク

296 a vast desert
|dézərt| ◀アク

297 climb a mountain
|kláɪm| ◀発音　|máʊntn|

298 a wide river
[wáɪd]

299 face the sea
|féɪs|

300 flat land
|flǽt|

100個 一気食いへの挑戦！

挑戦日	所要時間	正答数
1 年　月　日	分　　秒	/100
2 年　月　日	分　　秒	/100
3 年　月　日	分　　秒	/100
4 年　月　日	分　　秒	/100
5 年　月　日	分　　秒	/100
6 年　月　日	分　　秒	/100
7 年　月　日	分　　秒	/100
8 年　月　日	分　　秒	/100
9 年　月　日	分　　秒	/100
10 年　月　日	分　　秒	/100

繰り返しは無限の喜びである

英単語つれづれ草

英文法マニアではなくピー単マニアになれ！

　ご存知のように，英語は世界中で話されている言葉であり，世界の共通語としての地位を不動のものにしつつある。そんな中で，あなたには知っておいて欲しい事実がある。それは，この日本の中でさえも方言が多数存在するように，英語にも数多くの方言のようなものが存在するということだ。

　ある地域では「間違い」とされる言い回しも，別な地域ではむしろ「正しい」こともある。文法的にいくら正しいとされる表現であっても，「そんな風には言わない」と言われてしまえば，それはもう誤った表現でしかないという事実だ。

　だからこそ，英文法マニアになってはいけない。英文法は地域差が見られないような基礎事項をしっかりと習得するくらいでいい。それ以上の文法力は使っていく中で身に付けていけばいいと私は思っている。

　誤解のないように言わせてもらうと，基礎英文法は非常に大切なものだ。99％ではなく，100％身に付けて欲しいと思う。しかし，ネイティブスピーカーでも意見が分かれるような細かな英文法の学習は避けるべきだ。使えるかどうかわからない内容に時間を費やすくらいなら，ピー単で「使える」表現を身に付けていく方が，はるかに有効な時間が過ごせるであろうことは言うまでもない。

　英単語はうそをつかない。英単語はあなたを裏切らない。目指すべきは英文法マニアではなく，英単語マニアであり，ピー単マニアなのだ。覚えるだけでなく，どんどん使って，本当に使える英語力を身に付けて欲しいと，私は心から思うのだ。

英語は言葉だ，声に出そう！

America
Asia
capital
central
China
continent
entire
European
Indian
Korea
northern
ocean
region
side
south
southeastern
States
United
west
world

301 全世界
the en..re w...d

302 ヨーロッパ大陸
the Euro..an Con...ent

303 東南アジア
Sou...astern A..a

304 インド洋
the In...n Oc..n

305 中央アメリカ
Ce...al Am...ca

306 アメリカ合衆国
the Un..ed St..es

307 中国の首都
the ca...al of C...a

308 韓国
So..h Ko..a

309 西側
the w..t s..e

310 北部地方
a nor...rn re..on

日本語 / Japanese

CD 32

301 the entire world
|ɪntáɪər| ◀アク

302 the European Continent
|jùərəpíːən| ◀アク |káːntənənt|

303 Southeastern Asia
|sàuθíːstərn| |éɪʒə| ◀発音

304 the Indian Ocean
|índiən| ◀アク |óuʃən| ◀発音

305 Central America
|séntrəl| |əmérɪkə|

306 the United States
|ju(ː)náɪtɪd| |stéɪts|

307 the capital of China
|kǽpətl| |tʃáɪnə|

308 South Korea
|sáuθ| |kəríːə| ◀発音

309 the west side
|sáɪd|

310 a northern region
|nɔ́ːrðərn| ◀発音 |ríːdʒən| ◀発音

311	東海岸	the ea...rn co..t
312	全国	the wh..e n...on
313	市役所	a c..y h..l
314	都市部	an u..an a..a
315	彼の生まれた村	his na..ve vi...ge
316	すばらしい場所	a won...ful p..ce
317	湖のそばに	b. the l..e
318	公園の近くに	n..r the p..k
319	教会の方へ	to...d the ch..ch
320	坂の頂上	the t.p of a sl..e

0.1秒でも速く言えるように！

area
by
church
city
coast
eastern
hall
lake
nation
native
near
park
place
slope
top
toward
urban
village
whole
wonderful

CD 33

311 the eastern coast
|kóust| ◀発音

312 the whole nation
|hóul| ◀発音 |néɪʃən|

313 a city hall
|síti|

314 an urban area
|ɔ́ːrbən| |éəriə| ◀発音

315 his native village
|néɪtɪv| |vílɪdʒ| ◀発音

316 a wonderful place
|wʌ́ndərfl|

317 by the lake
|léɪk|

318 near the park
|níər|

319 toward the church
|tɔ́ːrd| |tʃɔ́ːrtʃ|

320 the top of a slope
|slóup|

#	日本語	英語
321	地下の穴	an under...und h..e
322	島を発見する	dis...er an i..and
323	消防署	a f..e st...on
324	公民館	a co...nity ce..er
325	地元の銀行	a lo..l b..k
326	ヨーロッパへ旅行する	tr..el to E...pe
327	しばしばイギリスへ行く	go to En...nd fr...ently
328	オーストラリアへの旅行	a t..p to Aust...ia
329	外国から帰る	re...n from ab...d
330	ツアーを解約する	ca..el a t..r

abroad
Australia
bank
cancel
center
community
discover
England
Europe
fire
frequently
hole
island
local
return
station
tour
travel
trip
underground

CD 34

321 **an underground hole**
[ʌ́ndərgràund] ◀アク   [hóul] ◀発音

322 **discover an island**
[dıskʌ́vər] ◀アク   [áılənd] ◀発音

323 **a fire station**
[fáıər]

324 **a community center**
[kəmjúːnəti] ◀アク

325 **a local bank**
[lóukl]

326 **travel to Europe**
[júərəp] ◀発音

327 **go to England frequently**
[íŋglənd]   [fríːkwəntli]

328 **a trip to Australia**
[ɔːstréıljə] ◀発音

329 **return from abroad**
[rıtə́ːrn]   [əbrɔ́ːd] ◀発音

330 **cancel a tour**
[kǽnsl]   [túər] ◀発音

大切なのはくり返すことだよ

repeat

across
airplane
airport
attendant
beach
boat
border
building
cabin
distant
flight
fly
miss
overseas
passenger
sand
seat
spot
tourist
view

331	海外へ飛ぶ
	f.y ove...as

332	飛行機に乗り遅れる
	m..s a fl..ht

333	国境を越えて
	ac...s the bo..er

334	飛行機の座席
	an ai...ane s..t

335	客室乗務員
	a c..in a...ndant

336	空港ビル
	an ai...rt bu...ing

337	客船
	a pa...nger b..t

338	観光地
	a to...st s..t

339	砂浜
	a s..d b..ch

340	遠くの景色
	a di...nt v..w

英語
English

CD 35

331 fly overseas
[óuvərsí:z]

332 miss a flight
[fláɪt]

333 across the border
[bɔ́:rdər]

334 an airplane seat
[éərplèɪn] ◀アク [sí:t]

335 a cabin attendant
[əténdənt] ◀アク

336 an airport building

337 a passenger boat
[pǽsəndʒər] ◀アク [bóut]

338 a tourist spot
[túərɪst]

339 a sand beach
[bí:tʃ]

340 a distant view
[dístənt]　[vjú:] ◀発音

今覚えたその単語が、未来へつながる光となる！

341	見慣れた光景
	a fam...ar si..t

342	すてきな写真
	a lo..ly pho...raph

343	温泉
	a h.t s...ng

344	港町
	a ha..or t..n

345	部屋を予約する
	re...ve a r..m

346	居心地(いごこち)のよいホテル
	a com...table h...l

347	旅行ガイドを雇(やと)う
	h..e a t..r gu..e

348	おみやげを買う
	b.y a so...nir

349	大学教育
	uni...sity ed...tion

350	大学教授
	a co...ge pro...sor

buy
college
comfortable
education
familiar
guide
harbor
hire
hot
hotel
lovely
photograph
professor
reserve
room
sight
souvenir
spring
tour
town
university

教育

日本語
Japanese

 CD 36

341 **a familiar sight**
|fəmíljər| ◀アク |sáɪt|

342 **a lovely photograph**
|lʌ́vli|　　|fóʊtəgræf| ◀アク

343 **a hot spring**

344 **a harbor town**
|hɑ́ːrbər|

345 **reserve a room**
|rɪzə́ːrv|

346 **a comfortable hotel**
|kʌ́mftəbl| ◀アク　|hoʊtél| ◀発音

347 **hire a tour guide**
|háɪər|　|tʊ́ər|◀発音|gáɪd| ◀発音

348 **buy a souvenir**
|sùːvəníər| ◀発音◀アク

349 **university education**
|jùːnəvə́ːrsəti| ◀アク |èdʒəkéɪʃən|

350 **a college professor**
|kɑ́ːlɪdʒ|　|prəfésər| ◀アク

英語 English

覚えた単語を使ってみよう！

Will you marry me?

cafeteria
campus
class
favorite
German
give
high
history
Japanese
junior
lecture
library
pupil
scholar
school
several
smart
staff
student
subject
teacher

351	講義をする
	g..e a le...re

352	ドイツ人の学者
	a Ge..an sch..ar

353	大学構内の食堂
	a ca..us cafe...ia

354	図書館の職員
	the li...ry st..f

355	中学校
	a ju..or h..h s..ool

356	日本史
	Ja...ese hi...ry

357	私の好きな科目（かもく）
	my fa...ite su...ct

358	利口（りこう）な生徒
	a s...t s...ent

359	数人の生徒たち
	se...al pu..ls

360	クラス担任（たんにん）
	a c...s te...er

勉強

CD 37

351 **give a lecture**
[léktʃər]

352 **a German scholar**
[dʒə́ːrmən]　[skáːlər]

353 **a campus cafeteria**
[kǽmpəs]　[kæ̀fətíəriə] ◀アク

354 **the library staff**
[láɪbrèri]

355 **a junior high school**
[dʒúːnjər]

356 **Japanese history**
[hístəri]

357 **my favorite subject**
[féɪvərət] ◀発音 [sʌ́bdʒekt] ◀アク

358 **a smart student**
[smáːrt]

359 **several pupils**
[sévrəl]　[pjúːplz] ◀発音

360 **a class teacher**

友達にも教えてあげよう！

361	学級活動
	a cla...oom act...ty

362	宿題を終える
	fi...h my ho...ork

363	技術を向上させる
	im...ve my s..lls

364	上級コース
	an a...nced co..se

365	数学の試験
	a m.th ex...nation

366	難(むずか)しい試験
	a h..d e..m

367	満点を取る
	get a pe...ct gr..e

368	テストに失敗する
	f..l a t..t

369	平均点
	the a...age s..re

370	つづりの間違(まちが)い
	a sp...ing er..r

activity
advanced
average
classroom
course
error
exam
examination
fail
finish
grade
hard
homework
improve
math
perfect
score
skill
spelling
test

英語 English

日本語
Japanese

CD 38

361 a classroom activity
[æktívəti] ◀アク

362 finish my homework
[hóʊmwɔ̀ːrk] ◀アク

363 improve my skills
[ɪmprúːv] ◀アク

364 an advanced course
[ədvǽnst] ◀アク [kɔ́ːrs]

365 a math examination
[mǽθ] [ɪɡzæ̀mənéɪʃən] ◀アク

366 a hard exam
[ɪɡzǽm] ◀アク

367 get a perfect grade
[pə́ːrfɪkt] [ɡréɪd]

368 fail a test
[féɪl]

369 the average score
[ǽvərɪdʒ] [skɔ́ːr]

370 a spelling error
[spélɪŋ] [érər] ◀発音

英語 English

マイペース，マイペース

become
belong
ceremony
classmate
club
common
draw
equal
follow
graduation
line
matter
mistake
number
rule
school
sentence
subject
uniform
write

371 よくある間違い
a co..on mi...ke

372 文を書く
w..te a se...nce

373 主題
a su..ect m...er

374 等しい数
an e..al nu..er

375 線を引く
d..w a l..e

376 規則に従う
fo..ow a r..e

377 学校の制服
a s...ol un...rm

378 同級生になる
be...e cla...ates

379 そのクラブに所属する
be...g to the c..b

380 卒業式
a gr...ation ce...ony

学校生活

CD 39

371 a common mistake
|káːmən| |mistéik| ◀ アク

372 write a sentence
|ráit| |séntəns|

373 a subject matter
|mǽtər|

374 an equal number
|íːkwəl| ◀発音 |nʌ́mbər|

375 draw a line
|drɔ́ː| ◀発音

376 follow a rule
|fáːloʊ| |rúːl|

377 a school uniform
|júːnəfɔ̀ːrm| ◀ アク

378 become classmates
|klǽsmèits| ◀ アク

379 belong to the club
|bilɔ́(ː)ŋ| ◀ アク |klʌ́b|

380 a graduation ceremony
|græ̀dʒuéiʃən| |sérəmòuni|

英語 / English

381	冬休み
	a wi..er va...ion

382	日記をつける
	k..p a d...y

383	ノートを貸す
	l..d a no...ook

384	教科書を借りる
	bo...w a te...ook

385	ペンをどこかに置き忘れる
	le..e a pen som...ere

386	英和辞典
	an E...ish-Japa...e dic...nary

387	乾(かわ)いた空気
	d.y a.r

388	青空
	a b..e s.y

389	暖かい日差し
	w..m su...ine

390	曇(くも)りの朝
	a c...dy mo..ing

やればできる！

air
blue
borrow
cloudy
diary
dictionary
dry
English-Japanese
keep
leave
lend
morning
notebook
sky
somewhere
sunshine
textbook
vacation
warm
winter

天気

🔘 CD 40

381 **a winter vacation**
[wíntər] [veɪkéɪʃən] ◀ アク

382 **keep a diary**
[dáɪəri] ◀ 発音

383 **lend a notebook**

384 **borrow a textbook**
[báːroʊ]

385 **leave a pen somewhere**
[líːv] [sámwèər] ◀ アク

386 **an English-Japanese dictionary**

387 **dry air**
[éər]

388 **a blue sky**

389 **warm sunshine**
[wɔ́ːrm] ◀ 発音 [sʌ́nʃàɪn] ◀ アク

390 **a cloudy morning**
[kláʊdi]

英語 / English

391	雨の午後
	a ra..y a...rnoon

392	雪が降る休日
	a sn..y h...day

393	激しい嵐
	a vi...nt st..m

394	美しい夕日
	a bea...ful s..set

395	満月
	a f..l m..n

396	涼しい気候
	c..l we...er

397	寒い季節
	a c..d se..on

398	大雪
	a he..y s..w

399	強風
	a s...ng w..d

400	暑い夏
	a h.t su..er

そうだ！ピー単があるじゃないか！

afternoon
beautiful
cold
cool
full
heavy
holiday
hot
moon
rainy
season
snow
snowy
storm
strong
summer
sunset
violent
weather
wind

日本語
Japanese

CD 41

391 **a rainy afternoon**
|réɪni|

392 **a snowy holiday**
|snóʊi|

393 **a violent storm**
|váɪələnt| ◀アク |stɔ́ːrm|

394 **a beautiful sunset**
|bjúːtəfl| |sʌ́nsèt| ◀アク

395 **a full moon**
|múːn|

396 **cool weather**
|kúːl| |wéðər|

397 **a cold season**
|kóʊld|

398 **a heavy snow**
|hévi| ◀発音

399 **a strong wind**

400 **a hot summer**

100個 一気食いへの挑戦！

挑戦日	所要時間	正答数
1 　年　月　日	分　　秒	/100
2 　年　月　日	分　　秒	/100
3 　年　月　日	分　　秒	/100
4 　年　月　日	分　　秒	/100
5 　年　月　日	分　　秒	/100
6 　年　月　日	分　　秒	/100
7 　年　月　日	分　　秒	/100
8 　年　月　日	分　　秒	/100
9 　年　月　日	分　　秒	/100
10 　年　月　日	分　　秒	/100

繰り返しは無限の喜びである

英単語つれづれ草

「悩む」と「深く考える」

悩むことはないですか？ もしあなたが悩むときがあれば，この言葉を思い出してください。「悩んでいても，きっと解決しない。」

私は昔，よく悩んでいました。いろんなことで悩むんですよね。膨大な時間を消費して悩むのですが，明確な答えは最後まで見つからない。それでも自分なりの結論を絞り出して行動してみるのですが，100％失敗する。少なくとも，私にとって「悩む」という行為はそのような時間の無駄以外の何ものでもない行為でした。

英語で「悩む」に相当する表現は数多くありますが，be worried（心配させられている）のような受動態（主語が動作を受ける形）や，suffer from（苦しむ）のようなマイナス表現を使います。つまり，受動的でマイナスな行為が「悩む」ということだと思うのです。

なぜ人は悩むのだろうと「考えた」ことがあります。なぜ悩むのか。それは，自分の今の経験や知識では答えが出せないからこそ，「悩む」のだと思うのです。ならば，悩むだけ時間の無駄。解決する唯一の手段は，前へ進んでいき，さらなる知識や経験を積んでいくしかありません。

よく「悩む」ことと「深く考える」ことを混同する人がいますが，深く考えるという行為は think 〜 over のような能動態（主語が動作をする形）で表現します。つまり，自分が望んでするプラスな行為が「深く考える」なんですね。

深く考えているならいいですが，自分が悩んでいると感じたら，それは気持ちを切りかえて，前へ進んでいくべきです。もう一度言いましょう。悩むのは時間の無駄です。さあ進みましょう，前へ！

英語 English

今日も元気だ，ピー単やろう！

401	屋外の気温 the ou...or temp...ture
402	傘を持ってくる b..ng an um...lla
403	緑色植物 g...n p...ts
404	赤いバラ a r.d r..e
405	黄色い葉 a ye...w l..f
406	迷子のヒツジ a l..t s..ep
407	かごの中の鳥 a b..d in a c..e
408	ウサギをつかまえる c..ch a ra..it
409	ねずみを殺す k..l a m..se
410	黒いクマ a b...k b..r

生物

bear
bird
black
bring
cage
catch
green
kill
leaf
lost
mouse
outdoor
plant
rabbit
red
rose
sheep
temperature
umbrella
yellow

CD 42

401 **the outdoor temperature**
[témpərtʃər] ◀発音 ◀アク

402 **bring an umbrella**
[bríŋ]   [ʌmbrélə] ◀アク

403 **green plants**

404 **a red rose**
[róuz]

405 **a yellow leaf**
[líːf]

406 **a lost sheep**
[ʃíːp]

407 **a bird in a cage**
[kéɪdʒ] ◀発音

408 **catch a rabbit**

409 **kill a mouse**
[máus]

410 **a black bear**
[béər] ◀発音

1日はピー単に始まり、ピー単に終わる			
	411	白い馬	a w..te h..se
	412	大きな牛	a b.g c.w
	413	アフリカゾウ	an A...can ele...nt
	414	ライオンを狩る	h..t a l..n
	415	トラの尾	a t..er's t..l
	416	クジラを守る	pr...ct w...es
	417	サルに関する本	a book a...t mo...ys
	418	熱帯魚	a tro...al f..h
	419	犬が好きだ	be f..d of d..s
	420	ペットの持ち主	a p.t o..er

about
African
big
cow
dog
elephant
fish
fond
horse
hunt
lion
monkey
owner
pet
protect
tail
tiger
tropical
whale
white

CD 43

411 a white horse
[wáɪt] [hɔ́ːrs]

412 a big cow
[káu] ◀発音

413 an African elephant
[ǽfrɪkən] ◀アク [éləfənt]

414 hunt a lion
[hʌ́nt] [láɪən]

415 a tiger's tail
[táɪgərz] [téɪl]

416 protect whales
[wéɪlz] ◀発音

417 a book about monkeys
[mʌ́ŋkiz] ◀発音

418 a tropical fish
[trɑ́ːpɪkl]

419 be fond of dogs
[fɑ́ːnd]

420 a pet owner
[óʊnər] ◀発音

英語 English

書いてみるのも忘れずに！

421	かわいい子犬
	a c..e pu..y

422	太ったネコ
	a f.t c.t

423	自然の美しさ
	na...al be..ty

自然

424	自然を守る
	s..e na..re

animal
approach
beauty
bottle
bucket
cat
cause
cute
damage
fat
garbage
natural
nature
plastic
puppy
save
ship
sink
typhoon
wild

425	野生動物
	w..d an...ls

426	ペットボトル
	a pl...ic bo...e

427	バケツ一杯(いっぱい)のごみ
	a bu..et of ga...ge

428	近づいている台風
	an ap...aching ty..oon

429	損害(そんがい)を引き起こす
	c..se da...e

430	沈(しず)んでいる船
	a s...ing s..p

101

CD 44

421 **a cute puppy**
[kjúːt] [pápi]

422 **a fat cat**

423 **natural beauty**
[bjúːti]

424 **save nature**
[séɪv] [néɪtʃər] ◀発音

425 **wild animals**
[wáɪld] [ǽnəmlz]

426 **a plastic bottle**
[báːtl]

427 **a bucket of garbage**
[bʌ́kət] [gáːrbɪdʒ] ◀発音 ◀アク

428 **an approaching typhoon**
[əpróʊtʃɪŋ] [taɪfúːn] ◀発音

429 **cause damage**
[kɔ́ːz] ◀発音 [dǽmɪdʒ] ◀アク

430 **a sinking ship**

英語
English

書いて，書いて，書きまくる

431	森林火災
	a fo..st f..e

432	固い木材
	h..d w..d

433	転がる石
	a ro..ing s..ne

434	氷のかたまり
	an i.e b..ck

block
discovery
fantastic
farm
field
fire
forest
grow
hard
ice
invent
machine
orange
rice
roll
run
stone
study
wood

435	農場を経営する
	r.n a f..m

436	オレンジを栽培(さいばい)する
	g..w or...es

437	稲田(いなだ)
	a r..e fi..d

438	すばらしい発見
	a fan...tic dis...ery

科学

439	研究分野
	a fi..d of s...y

440	機械を発明する
	in...t a ma...ne

103

CD 45

431 a forest fire
[fá:rəst] ◀アク

432 hard wood
[háːrd] [wúd] ◀発音

433 a rolling stone
[róulɪŋ]

434 an ice block
[áɪs]

435 run a farm
[fáːrm]

436 grow oranges
[ɔ́(ː)rɪndʒɪz] ◀発音

437 a rice field
[ráɪs] [fíːld]

438 a fantastic discovery
[fæntǽstɪk] [dɪskʌ́vəri]

439 a field of study
[fíːld]

440 invent a machine
[ɪnvént] ◀アク [məʃíːn] ◀発音◀アク

441 巧みな発明
a c...er in...tion

442 科学の時代
the sci...ific a.e

443 宇宙旅行
s...e tr..el

444 おもちゃのロケット
a t.y ro..et

445 太陽光発電
so..r p..er

446 地球の裏側
the o..er e.d of the e...h

447 音波
s...d w..es

448 自動車工場
a c.r fa...ry

449 よりよいシステム
a b...er s...em

450 健康的な生活様式
a he...hy life...le

自信がついたら消しちゃおう

age
better
car
clever
earth
end
factory
healthy
invention
lifestyle
other
power
rocket
scientific
solar
sound
space
system
toy
travel
wave

CD 46

441 a clever invention
|klévər| |ɪnvénʃən| ◀アク

442 the scientific age
|sàɪəntífɪk| ◀アク

443 space travel
|spéɪs|

444 a toy rocket
|tɔ́ɪ| |rɑ́:kət| ◀発音

445 solar power
|sóʊlər|◀発音 |páʊər|

446 the other end of the earth
|ə́:rθ| ◀発音

447 sound waves
|sáʊnd| |wéɪvz|

448 a car factory
|fǽktəri|

449 a better system
|sístəm|

450 a healthy lifestyle
|hélθi| |láɪfstàɪl| ◀アク

書くときにも声に出そう！

451	毎日の運動
□□□	d...y ex...ise

452	健康管理
□□□	he...h co...ol

453	ほとんど眠(ねむ)れない
□□□	can h...ly s...p

454	十分な睡眠(すいみん)をとる
□□□	get en...h s...p

455	眠りこむ
□□□	f..l a...ep

456	目を覚(さ)ましておく
□□□	k..p a..ke

457	早く目が覚める
□□□	w..e up ea..y

458	中指
□□□	the m...le f...er

459	奥歯(おくば)
□□□	a b..k t...h

460	肩(かた)の骨
□□□	the sho...er b..es

asleep
awake
back
bone
control
daily
early
enough
exercise
fall
finger
hardly
health
keep
middle
shoulder
sleep
tooth
wake

英語 English

日本語
Japanese

CD 47

451 **daily exercise**
[déɪli] ◀発音 [éksərsàɪz] ◀発音

452 **health control**
[hélθ] [kəntróʊl] ◀アク

453 **can hardly sleep**
[háːrdli]

454 **get enough sleep**
[ɪnʎf] ◀発音

455 **fall asleep**
[fɔ́ːl] [əslíːp]

456 **keep awake**
[əwéɪk]

457 **wake up early**
[wéɪk] [ɔ́ːrli]

458 **the middle finger**
[mídl]

459 **a back tooth**
[túːθ] ◀発音

460 **the shoulder bones**
[ʃóʊldər] ◀発音 [bóʊnz]

感情をこめて音読してみよう

461	白髪(しらが)
	g..y h..r

462	腕(うで)にけがをする
	h..t my a.m

463	首にけがをする
	in..re my n..k

464	足を骨折する
	b...k my l.g

465	ほとんど目が見えない
	ne...y b..nd

466	喫煙(きつえん)を許す
	a...w sm...ng

467	病気になる
	f..l i.l

468	病気の人
	a s..k pe...n

469	突然(とつぜん)の病気
	a su..en i...ess

470	インフルエンザにかかる
	c..ch the f.u

病気・治療

allow
arm
blind
break
catch
fall
flu
gray
hair
hurt
ill
illness
injure
leg
nearly
neck
person
sick
smoking
sudden

日本語 / Japanese

CD 48

461 **gray hair**
[gréɪ] [héər]

462 **hurt my arm**
[hə́ːrt] ◀発音 [ɑ́ːrm]

463 **injure my neck**
[índʒər] ◀発音 ◀アク

464 **break my leg**
[bréɪk] ◀発音

465 **nearly blind**
[níərli] [bláɪnd] ◀発音

466 **allow smoking**
[əláu] ◀発音 [smóukɪŋ]

467 **fall ill**
[íl]

468 **a sick person**
[pə́ːrsn]

469 **a sudden illness**
[sʌ́dn] [ílnəs]

470 **catch the flu**
[flúː]

最後にはすべてうまくいく		
	471	ひどいかぜをひいている
		have a b.d c..d
	472	ひどい頭痛がする
		have a te...ble he...che
	473	若くして死ぬ
		d.e yo..g
	474	死体
		a d..d b..y
	475	彼の鼻を検査する
		ex...ne his n..e
	476	医者にみてもらう
		s.e a do...r
	477	歯医者の予約
		a de...st a...intment
	478	入院する
		en..r the ho...tal
	479	看護助手
		an ass...ant n...e
	480	薬を飲む
		t..e me...ine

appointment
assistant
bad
body
cold
dead
dentist
die
doctor
enter
examine
headache
hospital
medicine
nose
nurse
see
take
terrible
young

日本語
Japanese

CD 49

471 have a bad cold

472 have a terrible headache
[térəbl]　　　[hédèɪk] ◀発音◀アク

473 die young
[dáɪ]　[jʌ́ŋ]

474 a dead body
[déd]

475 examine his nose
[ɪgzǽmən] ◀アク　　　[nóʊz]

476 see a doctor

477 a dentist appointment
[déntəst]　　[əpɔ́ɪntmənt]

478 enter the hospital
[éntər]　　　[hɑ́ːspɪtl]

479 an assistant nurse
[əsístənt] ◀アク　　[nə́ːrs]

480 take medicine
[médəsn] ◀発音◀アク

むだをこわがってはいけないよ

481	薬品箱 a d..g b.x
482	副作用 a s..e ef...t
483	前より元気になる g.t b...er
484	ゆっくりした動作 a s..w m...on
485	ボールを投げる t..ow a b..l
486	草の上に寝る l.e on the g..ss
487	一緒に働く w..k to...her
488	握手する sh..e h..ds
489	右手を上げる ra..e the r...t h..d
490	荷物を運ぶ ca..y the ba...ge

動作

baggage
ball
better
box
carry
drug
effect
get
grass
hand
lie
motion
raise
right
shake
side
slow
throw
together
work

113

日本語
Japanese

CD 50

481 **a drug box**
[drʌ́g]

482 **a side effect**
[ɪfékt] ◀ アク

483 **get better**

484 **a slow motion**
[móuʃən]

485 **throw a ball**
[θróu]

486 **lie on the grass**
[láɪ] ◀ 発音

487 **work together**
[təɡéðər]

488 **shake hands**
[ʃéɪk]

489 **raise the right hand**
[réɪz] ◀ 発音

490 **carry the baggage**
[kǽri]   [bǽɡɪdʒ] ◀ アク

114

だいじょうぶ，必ず覚えられるから

aside
bench
both
button
cry
full
ground
hand
lie
move
pull
push
quickly
rope
sit
slowly
speed
step
stop
walk

491 ゆっくり歩く
w..k s...ly

492 全速力で走る
run at f..l s...d

493 ベンチに座る
s.t on a b..ch

494 地面に横になる
l.e on the g...nd

495 泣きやむ
s..p c...ng

496 素早く動く
m..e qu...ly

497 わきへ寄る
s..p a...e

498 ボタンを押す
p..h a b...on

499 ロープを引く
p..l a r..e

500 両手で
with b..h h..ds

CD 51

491 **walk slowly**
[wɔ́:k] [slóuli]

492 **run at full speed**
[spí:d]

493 **sit on a bench**
[béntʃ]

494 **lie on the ground**
[gráund]

495 **stop crying**

496 **move quickly**

497 **step aside**
[əsáɪd]

498 **push a button**
[bʌ́tn] ◀発音

499 **pull a rope**
[róup]

500 **with both hands**
[bóuθ] ◀発音

100個 一気食いへの挑戦！

	挑戦日	所要時間	正答数
1	年　月　日	分　秒	/100
2	年　月　日	分　秒	/100
3	年　月　日	分　秒	/100
4	年　月　日	分　秒	/100
5	年　月　日	分　秒	/100
6	年　月　日	分　秒	/100
7	年　月　日	分　秒	/100
8	年　月　日	分　秒	/100
9	年　月　日	分　秒	/100
10	年　月　日	分　秒	/100

繰り返しは無限の喜びである

英単語つれづれ草

速読とは

　速読とは何だろう？　答えはもちろん「速く読むこと」だが，どのくらい読めれば速いのだろう？　1分間に5ページだろうか？

　もし，あなたが「1分間に5ページ読める」驚異の速読法を「通常の」英語学習の成果として求めるのであれば，それは不可能だとお伝えしなければならない。そのたぐいの速読は，日本人が母語である日本語で練習をしたとしても身に付けるのには相当な努力が必要とされており，容易に身につく力ではないと伝え聞く。

　外国語である英語でそのような力が習得できる確率は，宝くじで一等に当選するよりもかなり低いだろう。もしかしたら，「このツボを買えば英語が速読できるようになる」というツボを購入した方が，そのような速読ができるようになる確率としては高いかもしれない（仮に売っていたとしても，絶対に私は買わないが）。

　では，あなたが求めるべき速読力とはどんなものだろう？　目安の1つではあるが，おおよそ1分間に 150 words 程度をしっかりと読むことができれば，試験や日常生活で困ることはほとんどないだろう。つまり，とりあえずの目標は「1分間で 150 words が読めるようになること」ということになる。

　もちろん，速く読むことだけで内容がわかっていないのでは速読の意味がない。速読力は，たくさんの文章を読んだ結果，英語そのものに慣れるからこそ身につく力である。最初のうちは英文の内容をじっくりと味わいながら，読み物として楽しみながら，むしろ内容に重きをおいて読んでいって欲しい。楽しみながら読んでいれば，速読はいつの間にかできるようになっているはずだから。

501	花を摘む	p..k f...ers
502	腕を組む	c..ss my a..s
503	目を閉じる	c...e my e..s
504	口を閉じる[黙る]	sh.t my mo..h
505	耳をふさぐ	c..er my e..s
506	鏡をのぞきこむ	look i..o a m...or
507	カレンダーを掛ける	h..g a cale...r
508	ドアにカギをかける	l..k a d..r
509	彼女のほおにキスする	k..s her ch..k
510	彼の頭を殴る	st...e his h..d

続ければ結果はついてくる

arm
calendar
cheek
close
cover
cross
door
ear
eye
flower
hang
head
into
kiss
lock
mirror
mouth
pick
shut
strike

CD 52

501 pick flowers
[fláuərz]

502 cross my arms

503 close my eyes
[klóuz] ◀発音   [áɪz]

504 shut my mouth
[ʃʌ́t]   [máuθ] ◀発音

505 cover my ears
[kʌ́vər]   [íərz] ◀発音

506 look into a mirror
[mírər]

507 hang a calendar
[hǽŋ]   [kǽləndər] ◀アク

508 lock a door
[lák]

509 kiss her cheek
[tʃíːk]

510 strike his head
[stráɪk]

ピー単魂！

511	天井に触れる
	t..ch the ce..ing

512	ベルを鳴らす
	r..g a b..l

513	ろうそくを吹き消す
	b..w out a ca...e

514	皿を数える
	c...t p..tes

515	私のおばの趣味
	my a..t's h...y

趣味

516	有名な芸術家
	a fa..us a...st

517	油絵
	an o.l pa...ing

518	絵筆
	a p..nt b..sh

519	写真を撮る
	t..e a pi...re

520	家族の写真アルバム
	a f...ly p..to a...m

album
artist
aunt
bell
blow
brush
candle
ceiling
count
family
famous
hobby
oil
paint
painting
photo
picture
plate
ring
take
touch

CD 53

511 **touch the ceiling**
|tʌ́tʃ| ◀発音 |síːlɪŋ| ◀発音

512 **ring a bell**

513 **blow out a candle**
|blóu| |kǽndl|

514 **count plates**
|káʊnt| |pléɪts|

515 **my aunt's hobby**
|ǽnts| |hάbi|

516 **a famous artist**
|féɪməs| ◀発音 |άːrtəst|

517 **an oil painting**

518 **a paint brush**

519 **take a picture**

520 **a family photo album**
|fóʊtoʊ| ◀発音 |ǽlbəm|

さびしいときは、お風呂に入ろう

521	現代美術
	mo...n a.t

522	音楽を聞く
	l...en to m..ic

523	ピアノコンサート
	a pi..o co...rt

524	音楽の能力
	mu...al a...ity

525	ギターを練習する
	pr...ice the gu...r

526	歌うのが下手だ
	s..g b..ly

527	ヒット曲
	a h.t s..g

528	ロックバンド
	a r..k b..d

529	優秀な音楽家
	an exc...ent musi...n

530	バイオリンのレッスン
	a vi...n le...n

ability
art
badly
band
concert
excellent
guitar
hit
lesson
listen
modern
music
musical
musician
piano
practice
rock
sing
song
violin

CD 54

521 **modern art**
[mádərn] ◀アク

522 **listen to music**
[lísn]

523 **a piano concert**
[piǽnoʊ] ◀アク [kánsər(ː)t]

524 **musical ability**
[əbíləti]

525 **practice the guitar**
[prǽktɪs] [ɡɪtɑ́ːr] ◀アク

526 **sing badly**
[bǽdli]

527 **a hit song**
[sɔ́ŋ]

528 **a rock band**

529 **an excellent musician**
[ékslənt] [mjuːzíʃən] ◀アク

530 **a violin lesson**
[vàɪəlín] ◀アク [lésn]

お風呂上がりも,やっぱりピー単!

531	世界的なコンクール
	a world...e co...st

532	賞を取る
	w.n a pr..e

533	プロの歌手
	a pro...sional s...er

534	私のダンスの相手
	my d...e pa...er

535	ゆかいな喜劇
	a fu..y com..y

536	混雑した劇場
	a cr...ed th..ter

537	舞台の上に立つ
	s...d on a s...e

538	入場券売り場
	a ti..et co...er

539	映画ファン
	a m...e f.n

540	映画スター
	a f..m s..r

comedy
contest
counter
crowded
dance
fan
film
funny
movie
partner
prize
professional
singer
stage
stand
star
theater
ticket
win
worldwide

娯楽

CD 55

531 a worldwide contest
|wɔ́ːldwáɪd|

532 win a prize
|práɪz| ◀発音

533 a professional singer

534 my dance partner

535 a funny comedy
|fʌ́ni|

536 a crowded theater
|kráʊdɪd|　|θíːətər| ◀発音

537 stand on a stage
|stéɪdʒ|

538 a ticket counter
|káʊntər|

539 a movie fan
|múːvi|

540 a film star
|fílm|

| 英語 English |

テレビや映画を英語で見てみよう！

541	人気のある女優
	a po...ar ac...ss

542	テレビを見る
	wa..h te...ision

543	チャンネルを切り替える
	s...ch cha...ls

544	新聞を読む
	r..d a ne...aper

545	ラジオ番組
	a r...o pr...am

546	最近のニュース
	r...nt n..s

547	週刊誌
	a w...ly ma...ine

548	一般読者
	an or...ary re..er

549	テレビゲーム
	a v...o g..e

550	パズルを簡単に解く
	so..e a pu..le ea..ly

actress
channel
easily
game
magazine
news
newspaper
ordinary
popular
program
puzzle
radio
read
reader
recent
solve
switch
television
video
watch
weekly

日本語 / Japanese

CD 56

541. **a popular actress**
|pápjələr| |ǽktrəs|

542. **watch television**
|téləvìʒən| ◀アク

543. **switch channels**
|tʃǽnlz|

544. **read a newspaper**
|ríːd| |njúːzpèipər|

545. **a radio program**
|réidiou|◀発音|próugræm|

546. **recent news**
|ríːsnt|◀発音|njúːz|◀発音

547. **a weekly magazine**
|mǽgəzìːn|

548. **an ordinary reader**
|ɔ́ːrdənèri|◀アク

549. **a video game**
|vídiòu|◀アク

550. **solve a puzzle easily**
|pʌ́zl| |íːzəli|

英語
English

世界中の人たちと友達になろう！

adult
bookstore
cards
enjoy
fairy
fiction
horror
kind
magic
page
play
please
public
reading
science
secondhand
story
tale
three
turn
zoo

551 トランプをする
p..y c...s

552 一種の手品
a k..d of m...c

553 公立動物園
a p...ic z.o

554 読書を楽しむ
e...y r...ing

555 古本屋
a s...ndhand book...re

556 ページをめくる
t..n the p..es

557 科学小説
sc...ce fi..ion

558 恐ろしい話
a ho..or s...y

559 おとぎ話
a fa..y t..e

560 大人３枚ください。
Th..e a..lts, pl...e.

本

129

CD 57

551 play cards

552 a kind of magic
[káɪnd]

553 a public zoo
[pʌ́blɪk] ◀アク [zúː]

554 enjoy reading

555 a secondhand bookstore
[sékəndhæ̀nd]

556 turn the pages

557 science fiction
[sáɪəns] ◀発音

558 a horror story
[hɔ́rər] ◀アク

559 a fairy tale
[féəri] ◀発音 [téɪl] ◀発音

560 Three adults, please.
[ədʌ́lts] [plíːz]

561	彼女の２作目の小説
	her se...d n..el

562	アメリカ人の作家
	an Amer...n w..ter

563	有名な作家
	a well-k...n a...or

564	（スポーツ）ジムに入会する
	j..n a g.m

565	テニスコート
	a te..is co..t

566	リンクでスケートをする
	s..te on a r..k

567	室内スポーツ
	in...r sp..ts

568	野球場
	a b...ball p..k

569	泳ぐのが上手だ
	s..m w..l

570	プールに飛び込む
	j..p into a p..l

American
author
baseball
court
gym
indoor
join
jump
novel
park
pool
rink
second
skate
sport
swim
tennis
well
well-known
writer

同じやるなら，楽しまにゃソンソン！

CD 58

561 her second novel
|nάvl|

562 an American writer

563 a well-known author
|wélnóun| |ɔ́:θər| ◀発音

564 join a gym
|dʒím|

565 a tennis court
|kɔ́:rt| ◀発音

566 skate on a rink
|skéɪt|

567 indoor sports

568 a baseball park

569 swim well
|swím|

570 jump into a pool
|pú:l| ◀発音

英語 / English

文化

581	西洋文化 Wes...n c...ure
582	歴史博物館 a his...ical mu...m
583	人間 a h..an b..ng
584	上流階級 the u..er c..ss
585	危険な習慣 a d...erous cu..om
586	社会的な問題 a so..al pr...em
587	正式な指導者 an o...cial l..der
588	イギリス政府 the B...ish gov...ment
589	アメリカ大統領 U.S. pre...ent
590	発展途上国 a deve...ing co...ry

時には歌って気分転換

being
British
class
country
culture
custom
dangerous
developing
government
historical
human
leader
museum
official
president
problem
social
upper
Western

政治・経済

CD 60

581 **Western culture**
[wéstərn] [kʌ́ltʃər]

582 **a historical museum**
[mjuːzíːəm] ◀アク

583 **a human being**
[hjúːmən] [bíːɪŋ]

584 **the upper class**
[ʌ́pər]

585 **a dangerous custom**
[déɪndʒərəs] ◀発音 [kʌ́stəm]

586 **a social problem**
[sóʊʃl] ◀発音 [prɑ́bləm]

587 **an official leader**
[əfíʃl] ◀アク

588 **the British government**
[gʌ́vərnmənt] ◀発音

589 **U.S. president**
[prézədnt]

590 **a developing country**
[dɪvéləpɪŋ] [kʌ́ntri] ◀発音

英語 / English

自分を信じて自分を極めろ！

#	日本語	英語
591	成功している弁護士	a su...ssful la..er
592	法律に反して	ag...st the l.w
593	警察官	a po..ce o...cer
594	自転車を盗む（ぬすむ）	st..l a b..e
595	酔った男性（よった）	a d...k m.n
596	戦争をする [戦う]	fi..t a w.r
597	直接的な行動	di...t a..ion
598	強力な兵器	a po...ful w...on
599	勇敢な兵士（ゆうかん）	a br..e so...er
600	銃を撃つ（じゅう）（う）	sh..t a g.n

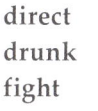

法律・治安

戦争

action
against
bike
brave
direct
drunk
fight
gun
law
lawyer
man
officer
police
powerful
shoot
soldier
steal
successful
war
weapon

CD 61

591 **a successful lawyer**
[səksésfl] ◀アク　[lɔ́ːjər] ◀発音

592 **against the law**
[əgénst]　[lɔ́ː] ◀発音

593 **a police officer**
[pəlíːs] ◀アク

594 **steal a bike**
[stíːl]　[báɪk]

595 **a drunk man**
[dráŋk]

596 **fight a war**
[fáɪt]　[wɔ́ːr] ◀発音

597 **direct action**
[daɪrékt] ◀アク

598 **a powerful weapon**
[páʊərfl]　[wépn] ◀発音

599 **a brave soldier**
[bréɪv]　[sóʊldʒər] ◀発音

600 **shoot a gun**
[ʃúːt] ◀発音　[gʌ́n]

138

100個 一気食いへの挑戦！

挑戦日	所要時間	正答数
1 年　月　日	分　　秒	/100
2 年　月　日	分　　秒	/100
3 年　月　日	分　　秒	/100
4 年　月　日	分　　秒	/100
5 年　月　日	分　　秒	/100
6 年　月　日	分　　秒	/100
7 年　月　日	分　　秒	/100
8 年　月　日	分　　秒	/100
9 年　月　日	分　　秒	/100
10 年　月　日	分　　秒	/100

繰り返しは無限の喜びである

英単語つれづれ草

あなたの知らない（かもしれない）世界

　あなたは学生ですか？　もしそうであるならば、あなたに伝えておかなければならないことがあります。あなたは知っているでしょうか。あなたが生活している「学生」と呼ばれる世界は、大人たちが創(つく)った虚像(きょぞう)の世界であり、学生の多くが、そのことに気がつくことさえなく、その虚像の中で生活をしているということを。

　学生という世界は「できる」か「できないか」で多くが判断されてしまう世界。「できる」ことがすばらしいことであり、「できる」ようになることを目標とする世界。その世界にいる間は、それが100％だと教えられることだろう。しかし、大人たちが生活する「社会」という世界では、その価値観は50％や30％でさえなく、0％になってしまうのだ。社会という世界では、「できる」のが当然で、ただ「できる」だけでは意味がない場合がほとんどなのだ。

　社会に入る、つまり就職するということは、「できる」人たちの集団に仲間入りするということ。つまり、「できない」という選択肢(せんたくし)はなくなってしまう。「できる」ことが前提(ぜんてい)になり、新たに「いつまでにできるのか」という処理能力(しょりのうりょく)も求められる世界になる。同じ仕事に、5日かかる人と、3日しかかからない人では、3日しかかからない人の方がより多くの仕事ができる。当然だよね。

　近年、必死に勉強して、やっと手に入れたあこがれの職業を「思っていた世界と違(ちが)う」という理由で、すぐに手放してしまう人がいるという話を聞いたことはあるだろうか？　思っていた世界と違うのではなく、そもそも「違う世界に入る」のである。そのことを、今から意識し、しっかり準備をしておいて欲しい。

では、処理能力を高めるためには何をすればいいのか？　実は、英語学習（他言語学習）は処理能力を高めるのに最適な方法の1つだと私は思っている。現時点では科学的根拠はないかもしれないが、私は高校生くらいまでは何をやってもノロマで本当によく注意を受けた。おまけに牡牛座だ。そんな私でも、（お世辞かもしれないが）今では「仕事が速い」と褒めてもらえることもある。しかし、私は他の人と特別違ったことを練習した覚えはない。唯一、必死になって練習をしたとすれば、それは英語学習しかないのだ。

　英語は勉強のグループに属するように見えるが、実はスポーツの特性の方が強い。例えば水泳だ。ただ泳ぐだけに見えるスポーツだが、基礎体力作りをし、1日に何千メートルも泳ぎ、同じ動作をくり返す中で精度を高め、結果を出す。

　英語も同じである。

　基礎体力とも言える単語や英文法を習得し、1日に何千回も音読し、すでに知っている知識を徹底的に反復することで完全に自分のものにしてしまう。そのような作業をくり返す中で、処理能力が少しずつ高まっていくと私は考える。

　もちろん、英語学習は相当な根気と努力が必要になる。しかし、その労力は、絶対にあなたの未来を切り開くための、礎を築き上げてくれるはずである。

　あなたが過ごす10年後の世界は、今の私が想像できる世界とは

全く違う世界かもしれない。しかし、どんな世界になっていたとしても、この能力は必ずあなたの味方になってくれるだろう。

　創られている世界の中で生活を送れるこの時期に、将来自分が世界を創っていく力を身に付ける。これは、「今のあなた」にしかできないことだとは思いませんか？

英語 English

千里の道も
ピー単から

branch
bring
business
clerk
company
copy
customer
high
international
office
open
own
papers
peace
position
service
shop
simple
task
those

601 平和をもたらす
b...g pe..e

602 国際的なビジネス　仕事・ビジネス
in...national bu...ess

603 会社を所有する
o.n a co..any

604 支社[支店]
a br..ch o...ce

605 店を開く
o..n a s..p

606 高い地位
a h..h po...ion

607 顧客サービス
cu...mer se...ce

608 それらの[あの]事務員たち
th..e c...ks

609 単純作業
a si..le t..k

610 書類をコピーする
c..y the p..ers

CD 62

601 **bring peace**
|píːs|

602 **international business**
|ìntərnǽʃənl| ◀アク |bíznəs| ◀発音

603 **own a company**
|óʊn|

604 **a branch office**
|brǽntʃ|

605 **open a shop**

606 **a high position**
|háɪ| |pəzíʃən|

607 **customer service**
|kʌ́stəmər| ◀アク |sə́ːrvəs| ◀発音

608 **those clerks**
|ðóʊz| |klə́ːrks|

609 **a simple task**

610 **copy the papers**

英語 / English

611	コーヒーの休憩(きゅうけい)をとる
	have a co...e b...k

612	短い休息を取る
	t..e a s...t r..t

613	英会話
	En...sh con...sation

614	適切(てきせつ)な語
	a s...able w..d

615	話題を選ぶ
	se..ct a to..c

616	率直(そっちょく)な論評(ろんぴょう)
	a fr..k co...nt

617	話し始める
	be..n to t..k

618	議論を始める
	st..t a disc...ion

619	早口でしゃべる人
	a f..t s...ker

620	声を聞く
	h..r a v...e

くり返し,くり返し,何度でも,何度でも

言葉

begin
break
coffee
comment
conversation
discussion
English
fast
frank
hear
rest
select
short
speaker
start
suitable
take
talk
topic
voice
word

CD 63

611 **have a coffee break**
[bréɪk] ◀発音

612 **take a short rest**

613 **English conversation**
[kɑ̀:nvərséɪʃn] ◀アク

614 **a suitable word**
[sú:təbl] ◀発音

615 **select a topic**

616 **a frank comment**
[kɑ́ment] ◀アク

617 **begin to talk**
[bɪgín]   [tɔ́:k]

618 **start a discussion**
[dɪskʌ́ʃən] ◀アク

619 **a fast speaker**
[fǽst]

620 **hear a voice**

一生使える英語力をつけよう！

621	退屈（たいくつ）な冗談（じょうだん）
	a bo...g j..e

622	うそをつく
	t..l a l..e

623	意思を通（つう）じ合える
	be a..e to co...nicate

624	コミュニケーションの手段
	a m..ns of communi...ion

625	外国語
	a fo...gn lan...ge

626	イタリア語を勉強する
	st..y Ita...n

627	スペイン語を教える
	t...h Sp...sh

628	韓国語（かんこくご）を習得する
	ma..er K...an

629	中国語を流ちょうに話す
	sp..k Ch...se f...ntly

630	声を出して詩を読む
	r..d a p..m a...d

able
aloud
boring
Chinese
communicate
communication
fluently
foreign
Italian
joke
Korean
language
lie
master
means
poem
read
Spanish
speak
study
teach
tell

英語 English

日本語 / Japanese

CD 64

621 a boring joke
[bɔ́:rɪŋ] [dʒóʊk]

622 tell a lie
[láɪ] ◀発音

623 be able to communicate
[kəmjú:nəkèɪt] ◀アク

624 a means of communication
[mí:nz] [kəmjù:nəkéɪʃən] ◀アク

625 a foreign language
[fɑ́:rən] ◀発音 [lǽŋgwɪdʒ] ◀発音

626 study Italian
[stʌ́di] [ɪtǽljən] ◀アク

627 teach Spanish
[tí:tʃ] [spǽnɪʃ]

628 master Korean
[kərí:ən] ◀アク

629 speak Chinese fluently
[tʃàɪní:z] [flú:əntli]

630 read a poem aloud
[póʊəm] ◀発音 [əláʊd] ◀発音

英 語
English

友達と競争するともり上がるぞ！

631	**正しい文法**
□□□	co...ct gr...ar

632	**易(やさ)しい表現**
□□□	an e..y ex...ssion

633	**言い換(か)えれば**
□□□	in o..er w..ds

634	**アルファベットを習う**
□□□	l...n the a...abet

635	**引用符(いんようふ)**
□□□	q..tation m..ks

636	**注意深い聞き手**
□□□	a ca...ul li...ner

637	**さよならも言わずに**
□□□	wi...ut sa..ng goo..ye

638	**本当に残念だ**
□□□	be re..ly so..y

感情

639	**本当にうれしい**
□□□	be t..ly g..d

640	**みんなを喜ばせる**
□□□	p...se ev...one

alphabet
careful
correct
easy
everyone
expression
glad
goodbye
grammar
learn
listener
mark
other
please
quotation
really
say
sorry
truly
without
word

CD 65

631 **correct grammar**
[kərékt] [grǽmər]

632 **an easy expression**
[íːzi] [ɪkspréʃən]

633 **in other words**
[ʌ́ðər]

634 **learn the alphabet**
[lə́ːrn] [ǽlfəbèt] ◀ アク

635 **quotation marks**
[kwoʊtéɪʃən]

636 **a careful listener**
[lísnər]

637 **without saying goodbye**
[wɪðáʊt]

638 **be really sorry**
[ríːli] [sɑ́ːri]

639 **be truly glad**
[trúːli]

640 **please everyone**
[plíːz]

150

そうそう、その調子だよ！

641	大喜びする
	be gr...ly p...sed

642	うれしい驚き
	a p...sant su...ise

643	ひどく悲しい
	be te...bly s.d

644	とても驚いている
	be v..y su...ised

645	全く意外だ
	be qu..e su...ising

646	興奮した気分で
	in an ex...ed m..d

647	わくわくする旅
	an ex...ing jo..ney

648	喜んで叫ぶ
	sh..t for j.y

649	深く感動している
	be d...ly m..ed

650	印象的な演説
	an im...ssive s...ch

deeply
excited
exciting
greatly
impressive
journey
joy
mood
moved
pleasant
pleased
quite
sad
shout
speech
surprise
surprised
surprising
terribly
very

CD 66

641 be greatly pleased
[gréɪtli]

642 a pleasant surprise
[plézn̩t] ◀発音 [sərpráɪz]

643 be terribly sad
[térəbli]

644 be very surprised

645 be quite surprising
[kwáɪt] ◀発音

646 in an excited mood
[ɪksáɪtɪd] [múːd]

647 an exciting journey
[ɪksáɪtɪŋ] [dʒə́ːrni] ◀発音

648 shout for joy
[ʃáʊt]

649 be deeply moved
[díːpli] [múːvd]

650 an impressive speech
[ɪmprésɪv] ◀アク [spíːtʃ]

651	料理に興味がある	be in...ested in c...ing
652	快感	a f...ing of p...sure
653	幽霊が怖い	be a...id of gh..ts
654	死の恐怖	f..r of d..th
655	お金の心配をする	wo..y about m...y
656	彼の怒った顔	his an..y f..e
657	スキーに夢中だ	be cr..y about sk..ng
658	彼女に恋をする	f.ll in l..e with her
659	興味を示す	sh.w an in...est
660	孤独な外国人	a lo...y for...ner

体調が悪いときは無理をしないで休もうね

afraid
angry
cooking
crazy
death
face
fall
fear
feeling
foreigner
ghost
interest
interested
lonely
love
money
pleasure
show
ski
worry

CD 67

651 be interested in cooking
|íntərəstɪd| ◀ アク |kʊ́kɪŋ|

652 a feeling of pleasure
|pléʒər|

653 be afraid of ghosts
|əfréɪd| |góʊsts| ◀ 発音

654 fear of death
|fíər| ◀ 発音 |déθ|

655 worry about money
|wə́ːri| ◀ 発音 |mʌ́ni| ◀ 発音

656 his angry face
|ǽŋgri|

657 be crazy about skiing
|kréɪzi| |skíːɪŋ|

658 fall in love with her

659 show an interest
|ʃóʊ| |íntərəst|

660 a lonely foreigner
|lóʊnli| ◀ 発音 |fɑ́ːrənər| ◀ 発音

英語 English

休憩も大事だよ。メリハリをつけて覚えよう！

661	失敗を後悔する
	re..et a fa...re

662	息子を誇りに思う
	be p...d of my s.n

663	明るい未来
	a br..ht f...re

664	偉大な科学者
	a g...t scie...st

665	お互いを愛する
	love e..h o..er

666	優しい心
	a k..d h...t

667	精神的な重圧
	me..al pre...re

668	だれも信用しない
	tr..t no...y

669	いつも陽気だ
	be a..ays ch...ful

670	親しげなほほえみ
	a fr...dly sm..e

always
bright
cheerful
each
failure
friendly
future
great
heart
kind
mental
nobody
other
pressure
proud
regret
scientist
smile
son
trust

CD 68

661 regret a failure
|rɪgrét| ◀アク |féɪljər| ◀発音

662 be proud of my son
|práud| ◀発音 |sán| ◀発音

663 a bright future
|bráɪt| |fjúːtʃər|

664 a great scientist
|gréɪt| ◀発音 |sáɪəntəst| ◀アク

665 love each other
|íːtʃ|

666 a kind heart
|háːrt| ◀発音

667 mental pressure
|préʃər| ◀発音

668 trust nobody
|trÁst| |nóʊbədi|

669 be always cheerful
|ɔ́ːlweɪz| |tʃíərfl|

670 a friendly smile
|smáɪl|

あなた、なかなかシブイですね

671	めったに笑わない
	se...m la..h

672	青ざめる
	t..n p..e

673	私の第一印象
	my fi..t im...ssion

674	幸福を願う
	w..h for ha...ness

675	奇跡(きせき)を信じる
	be...ve in a mi...le

676	信じられない出来事
	an unbeli...ble ha...ning

677	心変わりする
	c...ge my m..d

678	そう思う
	t...k s.

思考・議論

679	注意(はら)を払う
	p.y a...ntion

680	その場面を想像(そうぞう)する
	im...ne the sc..e

attention
believe
change
first
happening
happiness
imagine
impression
laugh
mind
miracle
pale
pay
scene
seldom
so
think
turn
unbelievable
wish

日本語 / Japanese

CD 69

671 **seldom laugh**
[séldəm]　[lǽf] ◀発音

672 **turn pale**
[tə́ːrn]　[péɪl] ◀発音

673 **my first impression**
[fə́ːrst]◀発音 [ɪmpréʃən]

674 **wish for happiness**
[wíʃ]　　　[hǽpinəs]

675 **believe in a miracle**
[bɪlíːv]　　　[mírəkl]

676 **an unbelievable happening**
[ʌ̀nbɪlíːvəbl]　　[hǽpənɪŋ]

677 **change my mind**
[máɪnd]

678 **think so**
[θíŋk]

679 **pay attention**
[əténʃən]

680 **imagine the scene**
[ɪmǽdʒɪn] ◀発音◀アク [síːn] ◀発音

158

| 忘れた単語もあるけど，けっこう覚えたなあ |

681	まだ決めていない	haven't de...ed y.t
682	他人を判断する	ju..e ot...s
683	賢明な判断（けんめい）	a w..e j...ment
684	愚（おろ）かな選択（せんたく）	a fo...sh ch..ce
685	不可能に思われる	s..m im...sible
686	ほとんど役に立たない	be a...st u...ess
687	私の基本的な考え	my ba..c i..a
688	正直な答え	an ho..st an..er
689	実践的（じっせんてき）な助言	pra...cal a..ice
690	最善の方法	the b..t w.y

advice
almost
answer
basic
best
choice
decide
foolish
honest
idea
impossible
judge
judgment
others
practical
seem
useless
way
wise
yet

159

CD 70

681 haven't decided yet
[dɪsáɪdɪd] [jét]

682 judge others
[dʒʌ́dʒ]

683 a wise judgment
[wáɪz] [dʒʌ́dʒmənt]

684 a foolish choice
[fúːlɪʃ] [tʃɔ́ɪs]

685 seem impossible
[síːm] [ɪmpɑ́ːsəbl] ◀ アク

686 be almost useless
[ɔ́ːlmoʊst] [júːsləs]

687 my basic idea
[béɪsɪk] [aɪdíːə] ◀ 発音

688 an honest answer
[ɑ́ːnəst] ◀ 発音

689 practical advice
[prǽktɪkl] [ədváɪs] ◀ アク

690 the best way

英語 / English

> 今の努力が未来をつくる！

common
condition
difference
difficult
expect
favor
interesting
likely
memory
notice
old
plan
point
program
promise
propose
remember
sense
succeed
support

691 彼の支援を期待する
ex..ct his su...rt

692 成功しそうだ
be li..ly to su...ed

693 違いに気づく
no...e a di...rence

694 常識
co..on se..e

695 興味深い点
an inter...ing po..t

696 その約束を覚えている
re...ber the pr...se

697 古い記憶
an o.d me..ry

698 難しい条件
a di...cult con..tion

699 計画を提案する
pr...se a pro..am

700 計画に賛成して
in fa..r of a p..n

CD 71

691 expect his support
[ɪkspékt] ◀ア ク   [səpɔ́ːrt] ◀ア ク

692 be likely to succeed
[láɪkli]   [səksíːd] ◀発音

693 notice a difference
[nóʊtəs]   [dífərns] ◀ア ク

694 common sense
[séns]

695 an interesting point

696 remember the promise
[rɪmémbər]   [práməs]

697 an old memory
[óʊld]

698 a difficult condition
[kəndíʃən]

699 propose a program
[prəpóʊz] ◀ア ク

700 in favor of a plan
[féɪvər] ◀発音

100個 一気食いへの挑戦！

挑戦日	所要時間	正答数
1　　年　月　日	分　　秒	/100
2　　年　月　日	分　　秒	/100
3　　年　月　日	分　　秒	/100
4　　年　月　日	分　　秒	/100
5　　年　月　日	分　　秒	/100
6　　年　月　日	分　　秒	/100
7　　年　月　日	分　　秒	/100
8　　年　月　日	分　　秒	/100
9　　年　月　日	分　　秒	/100
10　　年　月　日	分　　秒	/100

繰り返しは無限の喜びである

英単語つれづれ草

水平線までの距離を知っていますか？

　不安になるときはありませんか？　今はまだないとしても，これから先の人生の中で，不安になることがあるかもしれません。

　大きな大きな夢を持って。その夢は本当に大きくて。すごく遠くに感じられて。どんなに頑張ってもたどり着けなそうなほどに遠くに感じられて。本当に自分の夢は叶うのだろうか？　……と，不安になるときがあるかもしれない。そんなときに，この話を思い出して欲しい。

　あなたは水平線までの距離を知っていますか？

　海岸線に立って，あなたの目線の高さから，遙か遠くに見える水平線までの距離は，およそ 4.5km。あれほど遠くに見える水平線は，決して自分の力ではたどり着くことなどできないだろうと思えるほど遠くに感じられる水平線は，実は歩いてもたどり着けるほどの距離でしかない。

　どんなに遠くに見えるものでも，たどり着くことなどできないのではないかと諦めてしまいそうになるほど遠くに感じられるものでも，実際はそんなに遠くないこともある。だからこそ，信じましょう。「遠くない。遠くない。自分の夢が叶う日だって，きっとそんなに遠くない！」と。前を見て，一歩一歩進んでいけば，きっとたどり着けるはずです。

　だから信じて進みましょう。ピー単をマスターする日も，英語をマスターする日も，きっとそんなに遠くないと。

今日の10個は明日の100個より価値がある！

brief
clear
collect
data
detail
different
explain
explanation
express
fact
gather
information
object
opinion
private
sample
strongly
thanks
useful
view

701 違う意見
a di...rent v..w

702 私の個人的な意見
my pr...te opi..on

703 強く反対する
o..ect st...gly

704 感謝の意を表す
ex...ss my t...ks

705 詳細を説明する
ex...in the de..ils

706 短い説明
a br..f e...anation

707 明白な事実
a c..ar f..t

708 役に立つ情報
us..ul inf...ation

709 情報を集める
ga..er d..a

710 見本を集める
co...ct sa..les

CD 72

701 a different view
[dífərnt] [vjúː]

702 my private opinion
[práɪvət] ◀発音 [əpínjən] ◀アク

703 object strongly
[ɔbdʒékt] ◀発音 ◀アク

704 express my thanks
[ɪksprés]

705 explain the details
[ɪkspléɪn] ◀アク [díːteɪlz] ◀アク

706 a brief explanation
[bríːf] [èksplənéɪʃən]

707 a clear fact

708 useful information
[júːsfl] [ìnfərméɪʃən]

709 gather data
[gǽðər] [déɪtə]

710 collect samples

711	リストの一番下に	at the bo..om of the l..t
712	棒グラフ	a b.r gr..h
713	実際の例	an ac..al ex...le
714	事故の報告	an acc..ent re..rt
715	たぶん本当だ	m..be t..e
716	もしかしたら間違っている	pe...ps mi...ken
717	彼の成功を確信している	be s..e of his su..ess
718	重要性を理解する	un...stand the i..ortance
719	可能な解決法	a po...ble so..tion
720	限度を超えて	be..nd the li..t

いつもカバンには
ピー単を,
ありがとう

accident
actual
bar
beyond
bottom
example
graph
importance
limit
list
maybe
mistaken
perhaps
possible
report
solution
success
sure
true
understand

CD 73

711 at the bottom of the list

712 a bar graph
[grǽf]

713 an actual example
[ǽktʃuəl] [ɪgzǽmpl] ◀アク

714 an accident report
[ǽksədənt]

715 maybe true
[méɪbi] [trúː]

716 perhaps mistaken
[pərhǽps] ◀アク [məstéɪkən]

717 be sure of his success
[ʃúər] [səksés] ◀アク

718 understand the importance
[ʌ̀ndərstǽnd] ◀アク [ɪmpɔ́ːrtns] ◀アク

719 a possible solution
[səlúːʃən] ◀アク

720 beyond the limit
[biάːnd]

行動・対応

721	懸命に試みる t.y h..d
722	夢を実現する re..ize my d...m
723	過去の経験 p..t ex...ience
724	大変な名誉 s..h an ho..r
725	不注意な行動 a c...less be...ior
726	重要な役割を果たす p..y an i...rtant r.le
727	彼の努力にもかかわらず in s..te of his e...rt
728	ボランティア団体 a vo...teer g..up
729	ゲストにインタビューする in...view a g..st
730	自己紹介する int...uce m..elf

夢は近づいてこない。自分から近づかないとね

behavior
careless
dream
effort
experience
group
guest
hard
honor
important
interview
introduce
myself
past
play
realize
role
spite
such
try
volunteer

CD 74

721. **try hard**

722. **realize my dream**
 [ríːəlàɪz] ◀アク

723. **past experience**
 [ɪkspíəriəns] ◀アク

724. **such an honor**
 [ɑ́ːnər] ◀発音

725. **a careless behavior**
 [kéərləs] [bɪhéɪvjər] ◀発音◀アク

726. **play an important role**
 [ɪmpɔ́ːrtnt] [róʊl]

727. **in spite of his effort**
 [spáɪt] [éfərt] ◀アク

728. **a volunteer group**
 [vɑ̀ːləntíər] ◀アク [grúːp]

729. **interview a guest**
 [gést]

730. **introduce myself**
 [ìntrədjúːs] ◀アク

731	彼に質問する a.k him a qu...ion
732	素早い反応 a qu..k re..onse
733	すべてを受け入れる a..ept ever...ing
734	秘密を守る k..p a s..ret
735	幸運 a l..ky ch..ce
736	幸運な出来事 a f...unate e..nt
737	最悪の状況 the w..st s...ation
738	トラブルに直面する f..e t...ble
739	チャンスを逃す m..s a ch..ce
740	回復の望み h..e for r...very

求められたことより，さらに上を目指そう！

accept
ask
chance
event
everything
face
fortunate
hope
keep
lucky
miss
question
quick
recovery
response
secret
situation
trouble
worst

状況

CD 75

731 ask him a question

732 a quick response
|rɪspɑ́:ns| ◀アク

733 accept everything
[əksépt]

734 keep a secret
|sí:krət|

735 a lucky chance
|láki|

736 a fortunate event
|fɔ́:rtʃənət|

737 the worst situation
[wə́:rst] ◀発音 [sìtʃuéɪʃən]

738 face trouble
|trʌ́bl|

739 miss a chance

740 hope for recovery
[rɪkʌ́vəri]

741	必要な場合には
	in c..e of nece...ty
742	最終段階
	the f..al s..ge
743	長所と短所
	m..its and d...rits
744	彼の唯一の欠点
	his o..y f..lt
745	魅力的な外見
	an a...active a..earance
746	はっきり見える
	s.e c...rly
747	よく似て見える
	l..k a..ke
748	面白そうに聞こえる
	so..d like f..n
749	真剣な顔つき
	a se..ous l..k
750	大いに増加する
	in...ase g...tly

特徴・外見

変化

alike
appearance
attractive
case
clearly
demerit
fault
final
fun
greatly
increase
look
merit
necessity
only
see
serious
sound
stage

すごい！もう少しだね！

CD 76

741 **in case of necessity**
|nəsésəti| ◀ アク

742 **the final stage**
|fáɪnl|

743 **merits and demerits**
|mérəts| |dɪmérəts|

744 **his only fault**
|óʊnli| ◀ 発音 |fɔ́ːlt| ◀ 発音

745 **an attractive appearance**
|ətrǽktɪv| |əpíərəns| ◀ 発音

746 **see clearly**
|klíərli|

747 **look alike**
|əláɪk|

748 **sound like fun**
|sáʊnd| |fʌ́n|

749 **a serious look**
|síəriəs| ◀ 発音

750 **increase greatly**
|ɪnkríːs| ◀ アク

次はピー単
BASIC 1000に
挑戦だ！

751	拡大し続ける
☐☐☐	co...nue to g..w

752	悪化する
☐☐☐	g.t w..se

753	進歩する
☐☐☐	ma.e pr...ess

754	突然現れる
☐☐☐	app..r su..enly

755	丸い形
☐☐☐	a ro..d sh.pe

756	奇妙な形
☐☐☐	a st...ge fo.m

757	何も知らない
☐☐☐	k..w no..ing

758	だれかほかの人
☐☐☐	so..one el.e

759	私は忙しいので
☐☐☐	be...se I'm b..y

760	もし彼が生きているなら
☐☐☐	i. he is a..ve

alive
appear
because
busy
continue
else
form
get
grow
if
know
make
nothing
progress
round
shape
someone
strange
suddenly
worse

その他

英語
English

日本語 / Japanese

CD 77

751 **continue to grow**
|kəntínjuː| ◀ アク

752 **get worse**

753 **make progress**
|práːgres| ◀ アク

754 **appear suddenly**
|əpíər| |sʌ́dnli|

755 **a round shape**
|ráʊnd| |ʃéɪp|

756 **a strange form**
|stréɪndʒ| ◀ 発音

757 **know nothing**

758 **someone else**
|éls|

759 **because I'm busy**
|bɪkɔ́ːz| |bízi| ◀ 発音

760 **if he is alive**
|əláɪv|

176

英語
English

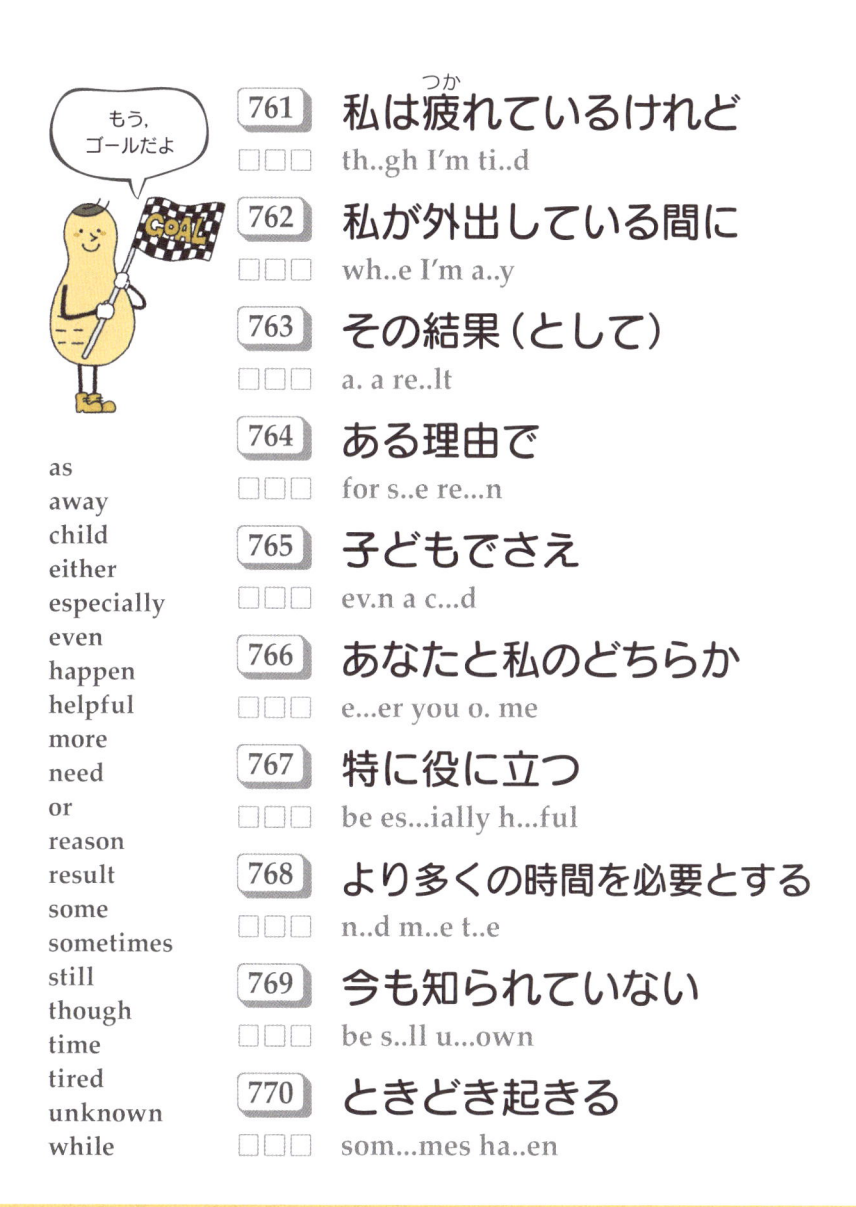

もう、ゴールだよ

761	私は疲れているけれど
□□□	th..gh I'm ti..d

762	私が外出している間に
□□□	wh..e I'm a..y

763	その結果（として）
□□□	a. a re..lt

764	ある理由で
□□□	for s..e re...n

765	子どもでさえ
□□□	ev.n a c...d

766	あなたと私のどちらか
□□□	e...er you o. me

767	特に役に立つ
□□□	be es...ially h...ful

768	より多くの時間を必要とする
□□□	n..d m..e t..e

769	今も知られていない
□□□	be s..ll u...own

770	ときどき起きる
□□□	som...mes ha..en

as
away
child
either
especially
even
happen
helpful
more
need
or
reason
result
some
sometimes
still
though
time
tired
unknown
while

日本語
Japanese

CD 78

761 **though I'm tired**
|ðóu| ◀発音 |táɪərd|

762 **while I'm away**

763 **as a result**
|rɪzʌ́lt|

764 **for some reason**
|ríːzn|

765 **even a child**
|íːvn| |tʃáɪld|

766 **either you or me**
|íːðər|

767 **be especially helpful**
|ɪspéʃəli|

768 **need more time**
|níːd|

769 **be still unknown**

770 **sometimes happen**
|sʌ́mtàɪmz| ◀アク |hǽpən|

178

英語 English

771 おもな目的
the m..n pu...se

772 どうして？
H.w c..e?

773 同じ意味
the s..e m..ning

774 あなたの親切のおかげで
t...ks to your k..dness

775 総量
the t..al a...nt

776 さまざまな種類の車
va...us t...es of c..s

777 私自身のやり方
my o.n s..le

やったね！自分をほめてあげよう

amount
car
come
how
kindness
main
meaning
own
purpose
same
style
thanks
total
type
various

CD 79

771 the main purpose
|méɪn| |pə́ːrpəs| ◀発音

772 How come?

773 the same meaning
|séɪm| |míːnɪŋ|

774 thanks to your kindness
|káɪndnəs|

775 the total amount
|tóʊtl| |əmáʊnt|

776 various types of cars
|véəriəs| ◀発音 |táɪps|

777 my own style
|óʊn| |stáɪl|

77個 一気食いへの挑戦！

挑戦日	所要時間	正答数
1 　　年　月　日	分　　　秒	/77
2 　　年　月　日	分　　　秒	/77
3 　　年　月　日	分　　　秒	/77
4 　　年　月　日	分　　　秒	/77
5 　　年　月　日	分　　　秒	/77
6 　　年　月　日	分　　　秒	/77
7 　　年　月　日	分　　　秒	/77
8 　　年　月　日	分　　　秒	/77
9 　　年　月　日	分　　　秒	/77
10 　　年　月　日	分　　　秒	/77

繰り返しは無限の喜びである

英単語つれづれ草

あなたには夢がありますか？

　私には夢がある。「世界中のみんなが笑顔で生活をする。」それが私の夢。こんなことを言うと，偽善者だと笑う人もいるかもしれない。でも，そんなことはない。確かに，私も心のどこかで自分だけが幸せならばそれでいいと思っているかもしれない。でも，自分だけが幸せでいることなど絶対にあり得ない。そう思いませんか？

　仮に，自分が最高に幸せな生活を送っているとしましょう。でも，目の前に，泣いたり苦しんだりしている人がいたら，その瞬間に自分の幸せな気分など崩れ落ちてしまうでしょう。自分が幸せでいるためには，自分の周りにいる人はいつも笑っていなければいけない。周りにいる人が笑うためには，その周りにいる人が笑っていなければいけない。そう考えると，世界中のみんなが幸せにならなければ，本当の意味で自分が幸せになる日は来ないのではないかと，そう私は考えている。

　もちろん，できることには限界がある。だからこそ，少なくともこうしてピー単を手に取ってくれたあなたには，心から幸せになって，笑顔で人生を送っていって欲しいと願っている。だからこそ，「学校の成績のため」とか「受験のため」とか，そんなくだらない，そのもの自体には石ころほどの価値もない，そんなものを最終目標に勉強をするのは本当に辞めて欲しいと願っている。

　あなたは，私たちは，もっともっと先にある，大切な夢を叶えるために必死で勉強をしているはずですよね。もしそうであるならば，本当に大切なものを決して見失ってはいけません。見失えば，そこへはたどり着けなくなってしまうのですから。

そして私は、夢を叶えるのに最も重要な力の1つが英語力だと思っている。少し前までは、「世界に出るなら英語」と言われていたけど、今はもうそんな時代ではない。街を歩けば外国の方はたくさんいる。世界を視野に入れた企業の中には、会社の中で使っていい言語は英語のみというところもある。外国の方がたくさん買いにくるからだと思うが、コンビニのアルバイト募集で「英語が話せる人」と書いてあったのを見たことさえある。

　だからこそ、今後の人生において、あなたがこの日本の中でのみ生活していったとしても、英語が必要になる瞬間は必ず訪れるだろう。そのときに、「あのとき、英語をやっておいて本当に良かったな」と、笑顔になってもらえたらと、私は心から願っている。

　もう一度だけ言わせてほしい。英語は学校の成績や資格試験や入試なんかのためにやるものではない。そんなもののためにやっては絶対にいけない。そんなものを目標にし、そこがゴールになってしまっては、あなたの努力は「無駄な努力」になってしまうじゃないか。英語は言葉であり、あなたの夢を叶えるための心強い仲間であり、世界中のまだ見ぬ友人に未来のどこかで出会うためのカギでもあるのだから。

　笑顔で、英語を、ピー単を。無限の可能性を秘めたあなたの未来のために。

おわりに

　かつて，日本では**必要以上の**文法学習に大きく力を入れていた時代がありました。「文法的に正しいか」は**誰**もが**研究**する一方で，「表現として正しいか」という最も重要な部分は多くの人が気にしない時代があったのは，**今では遠い昔の話**となりました。

　かつて，日本では**日本でしか教わらないような表現**を大量に授業で扱い，英語を母語として使う人たちでさえ知らないような**些細な違い**を，この上なく重要な内容であるかのように教えていた時代があったのも，**今では遠い昔の話**となりました。

　かつて，日本では単語を大量に覚えさせ，多大なる努力の末に覚えたにもかかわらず学生は全くそれらの単語を使いこなすことができず，教師はどんなに頑張っている学生に対しても**「努力が足りない」という見当外れの考え**を持っていた時代があったのも，**今では遠い昔の話**となりました。

　ピー単に出てくる表現は，表現として正しく，英語を母語として使う人たちが日常会話の中で，もしくは学校の授業などの中でごくごく自然に使い，意味を持った有機的な表現であるがゆえに，覚えたのに使えないということはあり得ない表現ばかりです。

　一度学習をし終えたあなたなら，ピー単が他の単語帳と似て非なるものであることは説明するまでもないでしょう。二度，三度と言わず何度も何度もくり返し，言葉としての瞬発力を徹底的に鍛えてほしいと思っています。そして，上記の「かつて」を，もっともっと遠い，誰も語り継ぐことがないほど遠い昔の話にして欲しいと，心から願っております。

INDEX

※数字は英文の通しナンバー

A

ability	524
able	623
about	417
above	294
abroad	329
absent	250
accept	733
accident	714
across	333
action	597
activity	361
actor	87
actress	541
actual	713
add	194
address	211
adult	560
advanced	364
advice	689
afraid	653
African	413
after	9
afternoon	391
again	24
against	592
age	59, 442
aged	83
ago	11
air	387
airplane	334
airport	336
alarm	233
album	520
alike	747
alive	760
all	23
allow	466
almost	686
alone	212
along	293
aloud	630
alphabet	634
already	28
always	669
America	305
American	562
among	286
amount	775
angry	656
animal	425
another	177
answer	114, 688
anything	166
apartment	213
appear	754
appearance	745
apple	201
appointment	477
approach	428
April	42
area	314
arm	462, 502
around	23, 277, 291
arrive	287
art	521
artist	516
as	763
Asia	303
aside	497
ask	731
asleep	455
assistant	479
attendant	335
attention	679
attractive	745
auction	122
August	45
aunt	515
Australia	328
author	563
autumn	36
available	123
avenue	266
average	369
awake	456
away	268, 762

B

baby	77
back	459
bad	471
badly	526
bag	96
baggage	490
bake	187
ball	485
banana	56
band	528
bank	325
bar	712
barber	247
baseball	568

basic	687	black	410	bus	282
basket	134	blanket	245	business	602
basketball	571	blind	465	busy	759
bath	237	block	434	butter	197
bathroom	241	blow	513	button	498
beach	339	blue	388	buy	348
bear	410	boat	337	by	317
beautiful	394	body	474		
beauty	423	boil	189	**C**	
because	759	bone	460		
become	378	bookstore	555	cabin	335
bed	236	border	333	cafeteria	353
bedroom	226	boring	621	cage	407
beef	200	born	88	cake	178
beer	175	borrow	384	calendar	507
before	8	both	500	call	113, 116
begin	617	bottle	176, 426	calm	210
beginning	40	bottom	711	camera	119
behavior	725	box	481	campus	353
behind	246	boxing	575	can	234
being	583	boy	258	cancel	330
believe	675	boyfriend	74	candle	513
bell	512	branch	604	candy	204
belong	379	brave	599	cap	159
below	295	bread	187	capital	307
bench	493	break	464, 611	captain	573
beside	236	breakfast	160	car	448, 776
best	690	bride	44	card	95
better	289, 449, 483	bridge	51	cards	551
between	168	brief	706	care	221
beyond	720	bright	663	careful	636
bicycle	269	bring	402, 601	carefully	275
big	81, 412	British	588	careless	725
bike	594	broken	238	carrot	188
billion	62	brother	81	carry	490
bird	407	brown	154	case	136, 741
birth	77	brush	242, 518	cash	95
birthday	178	bucket	427	casual	142
bit	165	build	216	cat	422
bitter	186	building	336	catch	408, 470

cause	429	closed	243	cost	99
ceiling	511	cloth	152	cotton	151
celebrate	37	clothes	141	count	514
cell	112	cloud	294	counter	538
cent	102	cloudy	390	country	590
center	324	club	379	couple	71
central	305	coast	311	course	364
century	38	coat	146	court	565
ceremony	380	coffee	611	cousin	82
chair	247	coin	101	cover	505
chance	735, 739	cold	397, 471	cow	412
change	100, 677	collect	710	crazy	657
channel	543	college	350	cross	270, 502
charming	149	color	130	crowd	286
cheap	106	come	772	crowded	536
cheek	509	comedy	535	cry	495
cheerful	669	comfortable	346	culture	581
cheese	190	comment	616	cup	177
chicken	174	common	371, 694	curry	185
child	765	communicate	623	curtain	246
China	307	communication	624	custom	585
Chinese	629	community	324	customer	607
chocolate	186	company	603	cut	190, 264
choice	684	computer	120	cute	421
choose	171	concert	523		
Christmas	37	condition	698	## D	
church	319	contest	531		
cigarette	136	continent	302	daily	451
city	313	continue	751	damage	429
class	360, 584	control	452	dance	534
classmate	378	convenience	103	dancer	50
classroom	361	convenient	129	dangerous	585
clean	157	conversation	613	dark	224
clear	707	cook	198	data	709
clearly	746	cookie	197	date	33
clerk	608	cooking	651	daughter	70
clever	441	cool	121, 396	daytime	32
climb	297	copy	610	dead	474
clock	29	corner	277	death	654
close	266, 503	correct	631	December	49

☐ decide	681	☐ dress	149	☐ enter	478
☐ deeply	649	☐ drink	98, 167	☐ entire	301
☐ delicious	184	☐ drive	271, 275	☐ equal	374
☐ demerit	743	☐ driver	281	☐ error	370
☐ dentist	477	☐ driving	274	☐ especially	767
☐ desert	296	☐ drop	94	☐ Europe	326
☐ desk	231	☐ drug	481	☐ European	302
☐ dessert	173	☐ drunk	595	☐ even	765
☐ detail	705	☐ dry	387	☐ evening	3
☐ developing	590	☐ during	32	☐ event	736
☐ diamond	109			☐ every	7
☐ diary	382			☐ everyday	135
☐ dictionary	386			☐ everyone	640

E

☐ die	473	☐ each	665	☐ everything	733
☐ difference	693	☐ ear	505	☐ exam	366
☐ different	701	☐ early	457	☐ examination	365
☐ difficult	698	☐ earth	446	☐ examine	475
☐ digital	119	☐ easily	550	☐ example	713
☐ dinner	163	☐ eastern	311	☐ excellent	529
☐ direct	597	☐ easy	632	☐ except	5
☐ direction	280	☐ eat	166	☐ exchange	111
☐ dirty	156	☐ education	349	☐ excited	646
☐ discount	97	☐ effect	482	☐ exciting	647
☐ discover	322	☐ effort	727	☐ exercise	451
☐ discovery	438	☐ egg	57	☐ expect	691
☐ discussion	618	☐ eighth	48	☐ expensive	107
☐ dish	172	☐ either	766	☐ experience	723
☐ distant	340	☐ elderly	260	☐ explain	705
☐ divide	193	☐ elect	573	☐ explanation	706
☐ doctor	476	☐ elegant	259	☐ express	283, 704
☐ dog	419	☐ elephant	413	☐ expression	632
☐ doll	137	☐ else	758	☐ eye	503
☐ dollar	61	☐ e-mail	118		
☐ door	228, 508	☐ empty	234	## F	
☐ double	58	☐ end	28, 39, 446		
☐ downstairs	227	☐ England	327	☐ face	299, 656, 738
☐ downtown	271	☐ English	613	☐ fact	707
☐ dozen	57	☐ English-Japanese	386	☐ factory	448
☐ draw	267, 375	☐ enjoy	554	☐ fail	368
☐ dream	722	☐ enough	454	☐ failure	661

fairy	559	fix	33	full	395, 492
fall	455, 467, 658	flag	579	fun	748
familiar	341	flat	300	funny	535
family	76, 520	flight	332	furniture	232
famous	516	floor	225	future	663
fan	539	flower	501		
fantastic	438	flu	470		

G

far	268	fluently	629		
farm	435	fly	331	game	549, 577
farmer	89	follow	376	garbage	427
fashion	150	following	20	garden	221
fast	619	fond	419	gas	273
fat	422	fool	42	gate	218
father	84	foolish	684	gather	709
fault	744	foot	292	gentleman	260
favor	700	foreign	625	German	352
favorite	357	foreigner	660	Germany	53
fear	654	forest	431	get	483, 752
February	40	forever	35	ghost	653
feel	164	forget	124	gift	110
feeling	652	fork	207	girl	257
fence	223	form	756	girlfriend	75
festival	36	formal	251	give	351
few	11	former	72	glad	639
fiction	557	fortunate	736	glass	175
field	437, 439	forty	65	glasses	147
fifth	41	fourth	43	glove	154
fifty	63	frank	616	gold	578
fight	596	free	98	golf	576
fill	240	French	172	good	183
film	540	frequently	327	goodbye	637
final	742	fresh	169	goods	104
find	140	Friday	5	government	588
fine	141	friend	255	grade	367
finger	458	friendly	670	graduation	380
finish	362	friendship	256	grammar	631
fire	233, 323, 431	front	219	grandfather	83
firm	256	frozen	265	grandmother	78
first	673	fruit	134	grape	181
fish	418	frying	199	graph	712

grass	486
gray	461
great	664
greatly	641, 750
green	279, 403
ground	494
group	728
grow	87, 436, 751
guest	729
guide	347
guitar	525
gun	600
guy	254
gym	564

H

habit	248
hair	461
half	16
hall	224, 313
hand	488, 489, 500
handbag	106
hang	507
happen	770
happening	676
happiness	674
happy	69
harbor	344
hard	366, 432, 572, 721
hardly	453
hat	158
have	161
head	159, 510
headache	472
health	452
healthy	450
hear	620
heart	666
heavy	398

height	50
helpful	767
here	291
high	355, 606
highway	263
hill	292
hire	347
historical	582
history	356
hit	272, 527
hobby	515
hold	115, 249
hole	321
holiday	392
home	220
homeless	215
homemade	203
homework	362
honest	688
honor	724
hope	740
horizon	295
horror	558
horse	411
hospital	478
hot	185, 343, 400
hotel	346
hour	16
house	216
how	772
human	583
hundred	64
hungry	164
hunt	414
hurry	289
hurt	462
husband	72

I

ice	434
idea	687
if	760
ill	467
illness	469
imagine	680
importance	718
important	726
impossible	685
impression	673
impressive	650
improve	363
increase	750
Indian	304
indoor	567
information	708
injure	463
inside	153
instead	85
interest	659
interested	651
interesting	695
international	602
Internet	122
interview	729
into	506
introduce	730
invent	440
invention	441
invitation	251
invite	75
island	322
Italian	626
item	135

J

| jacket | 144 |

January	39	last	22, 35	loose	144
Japanese	356	late	34	lose	138
jewel	108	later	25, 30, 116	lost	140, 406
join	564	laugh	671	lot	56
joke	621	laundry	157	loud	229
journey	647	law	592	love	658
joy	648	lawyer	591	lovely	342
judge	682	lead	574	low	60, 91
judgment	683	leader	587	lower	244
juice	202	leaf	405	lucky	735
July	45	learn	634	lunch	161
jump	570	leave	385		
June	44	lecture	351		
junior	355	left	276		
just	12	leg	464		

K

M

		lemon	192	machine	440
		lend	383	magazine	547
		length	51	magic	552
keep	382, 456, 734	less	65	mail	125
key	139	lesson	530	main	771
kid	215	letter	126	make	93, 753
kill	409	library	354	man	595
kind	552, 666	lie	486, 494, 622	manager	86
kindness	774	life	73	many	55
kiss	509	lifestyle	450	map	267
kitchen	209	light	162, 279	March	41
knife	206	likely	692	mark	635
knock	228	limit	720	marriage	69
know	757	line	115, 375	married	71
Korea	308	lion	414	marry	70
Korean	628	list	711	master	628
		listen	522	match	575
		listener	636	math	365
		little	13	matter	373

L

		live	212	May	43
lady	259	local	325	maybe	715
lake	317	lock	508	meal	168
lamp	231	lonely	660	meaning	773
land	300	long	21	means	624
language	625	look	139, 747, 749	meat	198
large	76			medal	578

☐	medicine	480	☐	mouth	504	☐	notebook	383
☐	meet	253	☐	move	496	☐	nothing	757
☐	meeting	250	☐	moved	649	☐	notice	693
☐	melon	193	☐	movie	539	☐	novel	561
☐	member	68	☐	much	93	☐	November	48
☐	memory	697	☐	museum	582	☐	now	12
☐	mental	667	☐	music	522	☐	number	374
☐	menu	171	☐	musical	524	☐	nurse	479
☐	merit	743	☐	musician	529			
☐	message	117	☐	myself	730			
☐	meter	66						

O

☐	middle	458				☐	o'clock	26
☐	midnight	27		**N**		☐	object	703
☐	milk	196	☐	name	82	☐	ocean	304
☐	million	61	☐	narrow	262	☐	October	47
☐	mind	677	☐	nation	312	☐	off	6, 90, 288
☐	mine	255	☐	national	579	☐	office	128, 604
☐	minute	17	☐	native	315	☐	officer	593
☐	miracle	675	☐	natural	423	☐	official	587
☐	mirror	506	☐	nature	424	☐	often	253
☐	miss	332, 739	☐	near	318	☐	oil	517
☐	mistake	371	☐	nearly	465	☐	old	697
☐	mistaken	716	☐	necessary	99	☐	Olympic	577
☐	mix	196	☐	necessity	741	☐	once	24
☐	model	150	☐	neck	463	☐	onion	191
☐	modern	521	☐	need	768	☐	online	123
☐	moment	14	☐	neighbor	230	☐	only	744
☐	Monday	1	☐	neighborhood	210	☐	open	605
☐	money	93, 655	☐	news	546	☐	opinion	702
☐	monkey	417	☐	newspaper	544	☐	or	766
☐	month	20	☐	next	1	☐	orange	436
☐	mood	646	☐	nice	254	☐	ordinary	548
☐	moon	395	☐	night	4	☐	other	446, 633, 665
☐	more	64, 768	☐	ninth	49	☐	others	682
☐	morning	390	☐	nobody	668	☐	outdoor	401
☐	most	67, 68	☐	noise	229	☐	outside	218
☐	mother	85	☐	noisy	230	☐	over	290
☐	motion	484	☐	noon	10	☐	overseas	331
☐	mountain	297	☐	northern	310	☐	own	603, 777
☐	mouse	409	☐	nose	475	☐	owner	420

P

package	52
page	556
paint	223, 518
painting	517
pair	131
pale	672
pan	199
pants	156
paper	132, 610
parent	80
park	318, 568
partner	534
party	249
pass	180
passenger	337
password	124
past	723
pasta	203
pay	92, 679
peace	601
pencil	130
people	67
pepper	195
per	18
percent	63
perfect	367
perhaps	716
period	21
person	468
personal	120
pet	420
phone	112
photo	520
photograph	342
piano	523
pick	501
picture	519
pie	201
piece	179
place	316
plan	700
plant	403
plastic	426
plate	208, 514
play	551, 726
player	571
pleasant	642
please	560, 640
pleased	641
pleasure	652
pocket	153
poem	630
point	66, 695
police	593
pool	570
poor	89
popular	541
population	53
porch	219
pork	174
position	606
possible	719
post	126, 128
poster	133
potato	189
power	445
powerful	598
practical	689
practice	525
precious	108
prefer	174
prepare	237
present	111
president	589
pressure	667
pretty	137
previous	74
price	60
private	702
prize	532
problem	586
professional	533
professor	350
program	545, 699
progress	753
promise	696
propose	699
protect	416
proud	662
public	553
pull	499
pupil	359
puppy	421
purpose	771
purse	138
push	498
put	146, 159
puzzle	550

Q

quarter	193
question	731
quick	732
quickly	496
quite	645
quotation	635

R

rabbit	408
race	574
radio	545
railroad	270
rainy	391
raise	489
raw	188
read	544, 630

reader	548	rope	499	send	118
reading	554	rose	404	sense	694
ready	163	round	755	sentence	372
real	109	rule	376	September	46
realize	722	run	435	serious	749
really	638			serve	172
reason	764	**S**		service	607
receive	125			set	205
recent	546	sad	643	seventh	47
record	117	safe	274	several	359
recovery	740	salad	207	shake	488
red	404	salary	91	shape	755
region	310	sale	97	sharp	206
regret	661	salt	195	sheep	406
remember	696	same	773	sheet	132
remove	208	sample	710	shelf	244
repair	217	sand	339	ship	430
report	714	Saturday	6	shoe	155
reserve	345	sauce	180	shoot	600
respect	80	save	424	shop	605
response	732	say	637	shopping	96
rest	612	scene	680	shore	293
restaurant	170	scholar	352	short	264, 571, 612
result	763	school	355, 377	shoulder	460
return	329	science	557	shout	648
ribbon	148	scientific	442	show	659
rice	437	scientist	664	shower	238
rich	88	scissors	131	shut	504
ride	269	score	369	shy	258
right	280, 489	sea	299	sick	468
ring	107, 512	season	397	side	309, 482
rink	566	seat	334	sight	341
river	298	second	18, 561	sign	278
road	265	secondhand	555	silent	113
rock	528	secret	734	silk	145
rocket	444	see	288, 476, 746	simple	609
role	726	seem	685	since	15
roll	433	seldom	671	sing	526
roof	217	select	615	singer	533
room	345	sell	104	single	73

sink	209, 430	soon	287	storm	393
sister	79	sooner	30	story	558
sit	493	sorry	638	straight	263
situation	737	sort	261	strange	756
sixth	46	sound	447, 748	straw	158
size	58	soup	184	street	262
skate	566	sour	181	strike	510
ski	657	south	308	strong	399
skill	363	southeastern	303	strongly	703
skip	160	souvenir	348	student	358
skirt	151	space	443	study	439, 626
sky	388	Spanish	627	style	777
sleep	453, 454	speak	629	subject	357, 373
slice	191, 192	speaker	619	subway	285
slim	257	special	173	succeed	692
slope	320	speech	650	success	717
slow	484	speed	492	successful	591
slowly	491	spelling	370	such	724
small	100	spend	31	sudden	469
smart	358	spite	727	suddenly	754
smartphone	140	sport	155, 567	sugar	194
smell	182	spot	338	suit	143
smile	670	spring	22, 343	suitable	614
smoking	466	staff	354	summer	400
snow	398	stage	537, 742	Sunday	7
snowy	392	stamp	127	sunglasses	105
so	678	stand	537	sunny	213
social	586	star	540	sunset	394
soft	204	start	618	sunshine	389
solar	445	States	306	supper	162
soldier	599	station	273, 285, 323	support	691
solution	719	stay	214, 220	sure	717
solve	550	steak	179	surprise	642
some	764	steal	594	surprised	644
someone	758	step	497	surprising	645
something	167	stew	200	sweet	182
sometimes	770	still	769	swim	569
somewhere	385	stone	433	switch	543
son	662	stop	282, 495	system	449
song	527	store	103		

195

T

- table 205, 235
- tail 415
- take 221, 227, 480, 519, 612
- tale 559
- talk 617
- tall 222
- task 609
- taste 183
- tax 92
- taxi 281
- tea 177
- teach 627
- teacher 360
- team 580
- teen 34
- telephone 114
- television 542
- tell 622
- temperature 401
- tennis 565
- terrible 472
- terribly 643
- test 368
- textbook 384
- than 25, 64
- thanks 704, 774
- theater 536
- then 15
- there 290
- these 105
- thick 245
- thin 152
- thing 55
- think 678
- third 225
- thirsty 165
- thirty 17
- this 2
- those 608
- though 761
- thousand 54
- three 560
- three-star 170
- through 284
- throw 485
- Thursday 4
- ticket 538
- tie 145, 148
- tiger 415
- tight 143
- time 768
- tired 761
- today 10
- together 487
- toilet 242
- tomato 202
- tomorrow 9
- tonight 26
- tool 129
- tooth 459
- top 320
- topic 615
- total 775
- touch 511
- tour 330, 347
- tourist 338
- tournament 576
- toward 319
- towel 239
- tower 29
- town 344
- toy 444
- traffic 278
- train 283
- training 572
- travel 326, 443
- tree 222
- trip 328
- tropical 418
- trouble 738
- truck 272
- true 715
- truly 639
- trust 668
- try 721
- Tuesday 2
- tunnel 284
- turn 276, 556, 672
- twentieth 38
- twenty 102
- twice 59
- twin 79
- type 776
- typhoon 428

U

- umbrella 402
- unbelievable 676
- uncle 214
- underground 321
- understand 718
- uniform 377
- United 306
- university 349
- unknown 769
- until 27
- upper 584
- upstairs 226
- urban 314
- use 241
- used 127
- useful 708
- useless 686
- usual 25, 248

V

vacation	381
various	776
vase	235
vast	296
vegetable	169
very	644
video	549
view	340, 701
village	315
violent	393
violin	530
visit	78
visitor	252
voice	620
volunteer	728

W

wait	14
wake	457
walk	491
wall	133
wallet	94
war	596
warm	389
wash	156
watch	84, 542
water	196, 240
wave	447
way	690
weak	580
weapon	598
wear	142, 147
weather	396
website	121
Wednesday	3
week	19
weekend	31
weekly	547
weight	52
welcome	252
well	90, 569
well-known	563
west	309
Western	581
wet	239
whale	416
while	13, 762
white	411
whole	312
wide	298
wife	86
wild	425
win	532
wind	399
window	243
wine	176
winter	381
wise	683
wish	674
within	19
without	637
woman	261
wonderful	316
wood	432
wooden	232
word	614, 633
work	487
world	301
worldwide	531
worry	655
worse	752
worst	737
wrap	110
write	372
writer	562
wrong	211

Y

year	23, 54
yellow	405
yen	62, 101
yesterday	8
yet	681
young	473

Z

zero	66
zoo	553

大岩 秀樹(Oiwa Hideki)
東進ハイスクール・東進衛星予備校講師。大学受験の勉強を始めた頃は英語を大の苦手としていたが、進学が決まった3日後には塾の教壇に立ち、英語の指導を始められるほどに成長。その後、23歳で衛星放送を通じて発信される授業の担当講師に大抜擢され、現在は中学生〜大学生を対象とする数多くの講座を担当。そのわかりやすく、ていねいな授業は幅広い層から支持されている。著書は「大岩のいちばんはじめの英文法 超基礎文法編」(東進ブックス)など多数。

佐藤 誠司(Sato Seishi)
東京大学文学部英文科卒。広島県教育委員会事務局、私立中学・高校教諭、予備校講師などを経て、現在は(有)佐藤教育研究所を主宰。英語学習全般の著作活動を行っている。著書に「入試英文法マニュアル」(南雲堂)、「英作文のためのやさしい英文法」「高校生のための英語学習ガイドブック」(いずれも岩波ジュニア新書)、「〈対訳つき〉シャーロック・ホームズの冒険」(PHP文庫)など。共著書に「アトラス総合英語」(桐原書店)、「中学英語を5日間でやり直す本」「英語力テスト1000」(いずれもPHP文庫)、「超整理！新TOEICテストビジュアル英単語」(ジャパンタイムズ)など。広島県福山市在住。

英単語ピーナツ JUNIOR　CD付

2014年4月30日　1刷
2023年7月31日　6刷

著　者	大　岩　秀　樹
	佐　藤　誠　司
発行者	南　雲　一　範
印刷所	日本ハイコム株式会社
製本所	有限会社松村製本所
発行所	株式会社　南　雲　堂

東京都新宿区山吹町361番地／〒162-0801
振替口座・00160-0-46863
TEL (03) 3268-2311　FAX (03) 3260-5425
E-mail：nanundo@post.email.ne.jp
URL：https://www.nanun-do.co.jp

乱丁・落丁本はご面倒ですが小社通販係宛ご送付下さい。
送料小社負担にてお取替えいたします。

Printed in Japan　(検印省略)

ISBN978-4-523-25157-6　C7082　<G-157>

学習に便利な『日本語→英語』の音声を
ダウンロード販売中！　定価400円＋税

Nan'Un-Do STORE
https://nanundo.stores.jp/　🏠STORES jp

『英単語ピーナツ』でサイト内検索！

英単語ピーナツ JUNIOR

英単語ピーナツJUNIORを
修了されたあなたには

史上最高のコラボ完成!!
安河内哲也×英単語ピーナツ

センター試験からやり直しまで

英語はピー単を音読しろ!

英単語ピーナツ
BASIC 1000

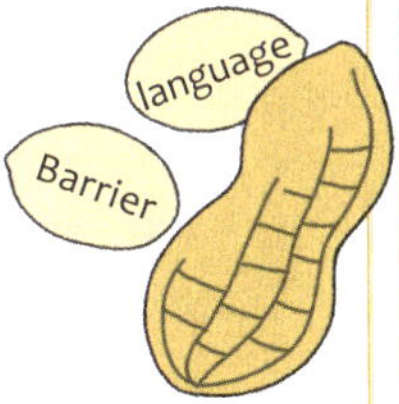

CD Book

language
Barrier

安河内哲也
佐藤誠司　共著

● 英語学参・語学書
● 四六判／280ページ

ISBN978-4-523-25156-9 C7082　定価（本体980円＋税）

まだまだ続く、
BASICコースを
英単語ピーナツほど
元祖!!
おいしいものはない

清水かつぞー
著

東大生もみんな読んでいた!?

全国の書店にて絶賛発売中！

英単語探求の道!!
修了された方は!!

金 Going for the Gold

メダルコース 【改訂新版】フルカラー
ISBN978-4-523-25155-2 C7082

銀 Going for the Silver

メダルコース 【改訂新版】フルカラー
ISBN978-4-523-25154-5 C7082

銅 Going for the Bronze

メダルコース 【改訂新版】フルカラー
ISBN978-4-523-25153-8 C7082

CD Book　各定価（本体 1,000 円＋税）

同時通訳の神様　國弘正雄先生推薦!!
東進ハイスクール　安河内哲也先生大推薦!!

小学校からの英語学習！
書いておぼえる はじめての 英単語ピーナツ

一粒にいくつも豆が入っているピーナツのように英単語はかたまりで覚えよう！

東進ハイスクール・中学NET講師
Z会進学教室 講師　　　　杉山一志
佐藤教育研究所 主宰　　　佐藤誠司　共著

ISBN978-4-523-26530-6 C6082　定価（本体1,200円＋税）

株式会社 南雲堂　〒162-0801　東京都新宿区山吹町361
http://www.nanun-do.co.jp/